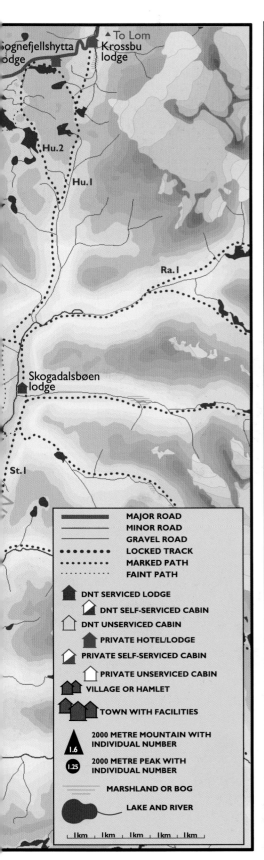

HURR... ...N)

1.1	**St...** (St...		
1.15			
1.16			
1.17	Skagastølsnebbet	2222m	
1.18	Nordre Skagastølstind	2167m	
1.2	**Styggedalstind**		**2387m**
1.3	**Gjertvasstind**		**2351m**
1.4	**Sentraltind**		**2348m**
1.19	Nordre Maradalstind	2160m	
1.5	**Austanbotntind**		**2204m**
1.20	Søre Austanbotntind	2103m	
1.21	Vestre Austanbotntind	2100m	
1.6	**Dyrhaugstind**		**2147m**
1.22	Søre Dyrhaugstind	2072m	
1.23	Nordre Midtmaradalstind	2062m	
1.7	**Store Ringstind**		**2124m**
1.8	**Soleibotntind**		**2083m**
1.24	Søre Soleibotntind	2049m	
1.25	Nordre Soleibotntind	2030m	
1.9	**Fannaråken**		**2068m**
1.10	**Midtmaradalstind**		**2056m**
1.11	**Stølsmaradalstind**		**2026m**
1.12	**Steindalsnosi**		**2025m**
1.13	**Midtre Ringstind**		**2025m**
1.14	**Østre Ringstind**		**2002m**

Store Skagastølstind from Midtmaradalstind.

This book is dedicated to:

My parents, Peter and Elizabeth Baxter, for their inspiration and unconditional support. Arne Instebø for his companionship in the mountains. Toby Curnow; he knows why. Bronwen Jeans for her patience and understanding while I was holed up writing this book.

Vettisfossen waterfall from Stølsmaradalen cabin.

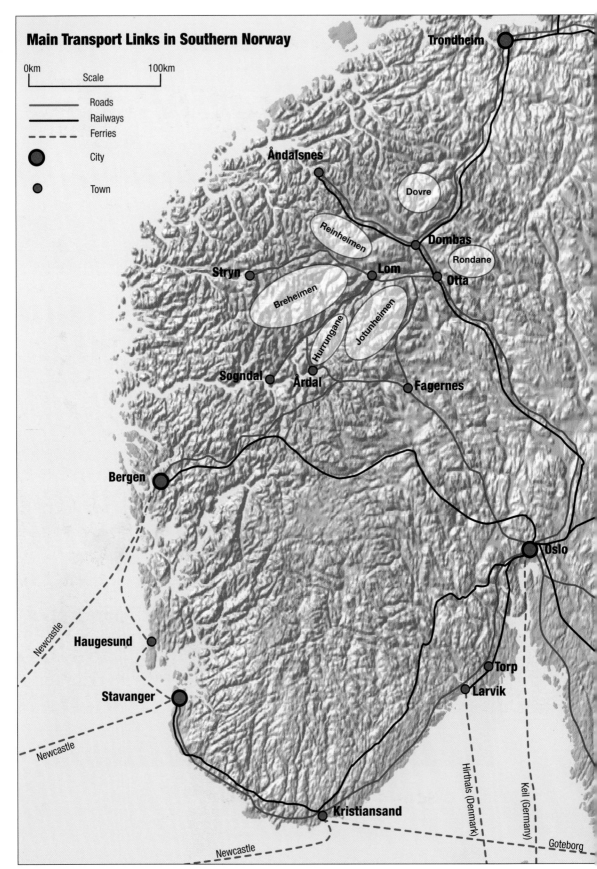

Main Transport Links in Southern Norway

0km — 100km
Scale

Roads
Railways
Ferries
● City
● Town

Trondheim

Åndalsnes

Dovre

Reinheimen

Dombas

Lom

Rondane

Stryn

Otta

Breheimen

Hurrungane

Jotunheimen

Sogndal

Årdal

Fagernes

Bergen

Oslo

Newcastle

Haugesund

Torp

Stavanger

Larvik

Newcastle

Hirthals (Denmark)

Keil (Germany)

Kristiansand

Newcastle

Goteborg

2

SCANDINAVIAN MOUNTAINS AND PEAKS OVER 2000 METRES IN THE

HURRUNGANE

Written by

James Baxter

WALKS, SCRAMBLES, CLIMBS AND SKI TOURS IN SCANDINAVIA'S MOST SPECTACULAR MOUNTAINS

Austanbotntind from Store Ringstind.

SCANDINAVIAN PUBLISHING
EDINBURGH

ISBN   0-9550497-0-9

Bar code number 9 780955 049705

Text, illustrations and maps © James Baxter 2005

First edition

Published by:
Scandinavian Publishing,
151 Bruntsfield Place,
Edinburgh,
EH10 4EB.

Printed and bound in Edinburgh.

Layout, maps and design by James Baxter and Steve Walsh.

Imaging by bmb Digital Imaging, Edinburgh.

All photographs outside flora and fauna section by James Baxter except:
Page 23/back cover - Arne Instebø;
Page 12 (left) - Bronwen Jeans;
Page 71 (lower) - Krister Jonnson;
Back cover of author - Tone Svødsnes;
Photographs from the flora and fauna section are by various photographers.

Distributed by:
Cordee Ltd,
3a de Montfort Street,
Leicester,
LE1 7HD.

We have made every effort to ensure the accuracy of this guide. However, phone numbers, bus times, logistics and even the landscape and climate are changing, which may compromise this accuracy. We therefore welcome any feedback you may have. If you should require any further information about Scandinavia we will be happy to help. Please Email your comments or queries to:
info@scandinavianmountains.com

Western half of the Hurrungane Massif seen from Stølsnosi on the Midtmaradals ridge.

Front cover: Styggedals ridge and Skagastøls ridge from Galdhøpiggen.

Back cover from top: 1. Austanbotntind from Store Ringstind. 2. Midtre and Store Ringstind from Ringsdalen.
3. Stølsmaradalen cabin. 4. Store Skagastølstind from Halls hammar. 5. Author: James Baxter.

CONTENTS

INTRODUCTION TO HURRUNGANE

A panorama of the southern half of Hurrungane from Langeskavlstind to the east. To see the identity of the mountains please refer to the map inside the front or back covers.

SCANDINAVIAN MOUNTAINS

Scandinavia has a wealth of spectacular mountains. Though only half the height of the Alps and not quite on the same scale of grandeur, they can match the Alps in almost every other respect. In Romsdal in Norway is Trollvegen, the highest vertical wall in Europe at 1700m. Between the largest fjords in the world on Norway's west coast are the largest glaciers in Europe. Sarek National Park in north Sweden is by far the greatest wilderness area of Europe. Indeed, the mountainous areas of Scandinavia are much larger than the Alps and Pyrenees put together.

Scandinavia has a richer selection of wildlife than the Alps or Pyrenees. Due also to Scandinavia's more northerly location, the seasonal variations are more extreme and interesting. For example, an area that is -30 celsius on a dark snowy January will be a lush meadow basking in +30 celsius under the midnight sun six months later. There is also a much more interesting variety of landscape including coast, fjord, forest, lake, alpine peak, glacier and tundra, most of which can be found in any given area.

While it is difficult to avoid the crowds in the Alps, Scandinavian mountains are by comparison almost deserted. The exploitation of and intrusion into Scandinavian mountain areas by tourism, industry and roads are negligible. In the more mountainous regions traditional farming and culture is still ensconced in Scandinavia and remain very idyllic. The industrial revolution which alienated most lower European countries from rural life never had much impact in Scandinavia. While the Alps rush to develop further, Scandinavians proudly try to preserve their rich heritage.

Scandinavia therefore has much to commend it from landscape, wildlife and cultural aspects. This book looks at just one aspect and one area of this fabulous land, namely the mountains over 2000m in the Hurrungane area. Unfortunately, this omits other fantastic mountainous areas like the rest of Jotunheimen, the Sunnmøre Alps, Romsdal, Innerdal, the Lofoten Islands, the Lyngen Alps and Sarek, to

name just a few, all of which contain superb mountain ranges that would be a Mecca if they existed in central Europe.

GEOGRAPHY AND GEOLOGY

Hurrungane is, geologically and in character, part of the Jotunheimen range found in central Norway. The Jotunheimen is the highest and grandest of all mountain ranges in Scandinavia, and arguably the most spectacular. One hundred and one of the 137 mountains over 2000m in Scandinavia are found in the Jotunheimen, which can be divided into 14 separate areas or massifs (see page 68-71). One of these 14 regions, Hurrungane, lies on the very western periphery of Jotunheimen, separated from the main area by the huge glacier-carved canyon of Utladalen. Hurrungane is the most alpine of all the 14 regions. Indeed it is probably the most alpine region in Scandinavia, and certainly the most alpine of all the regions where the mountains exceed 2000m.

Hurrungane, along with the rest of Norway and Scotland, is largely composed of very old rock formed some 400 million years ago when the Caledonian mountain range was thrust up. The enormous mountains created at this time were much higher than anything today but were completly levelled over some 100 million years into a flat plateau. This plateau remained from about 300 million years ago to 50 million years ago when there was more movement and the west side of the Scandinavian plate was heaved up just off the coast of Norway, while the east side remained lower. The whole plate was therefore at an angle, with the west side much higher than the east and all the rivers consequently flowing east.

Since this tilting of the plate some 50 million years ago there have been numerous ice ages which have eroded it, particularly the western higher side. In the last 2.5 million years it is estimated there have been some 40 different ice ages alone. These ice ages have been the main shapers of the landscape we see today as the glaciers which came and went scraped away corries and valleys, often leaving the higher peaks protruding through the ice. The last of these ice ages was from 50,000 years ago to 10,000 years ago, and this pretty much obliterated all evidence from the previous ice ages. There have been some minor ice ages since then, and even as recently as the mid 18th century there was a mini ice age when glaciers surged forward again, enveloping farms and fields. The scars from this age are still visible, as lichens are still recolonizing the recently exposed surfaces.

Geologically Jotunheimen is a distinct region composed of gabbro or gabbrogneiss rock varieties. The former is a very hard rough rock usually black with white flecks, and the latter is even harder and usually white with black flecks in parallel stripes. To the northwest lies the neighbouring Breheimen region which is largely composed of gneiss and to the east lies the neighbouring Rondane region composed of sparagmite, a softer sedimentary sandstone.

The gabbros of Jotunheimen, and especially Hurrungane, are a very hard resistant type. Despite seeing far greater glacial activity than areas further east (due to the greater precipitation on the western ranges) the hard rocks in Jotunheimen, and especially Hurrungane, have been stubborn in resisting glacial erosion. This has encouraged high angular peaks, often formed as the tops of these mountains pierced through the various ice sheets as nunataks. These high peaks are supported by arêtes formed by the glaciers scouring the sides of ridges until they narrow into sharp jagged buttresses.

Once the ice has scoured the ridges and corries it flows into primary glaciers, taking with it the debris which it has ripped from the rock and which has fallen onto it from the frost shattered summits above. These primary glaciers are an abrasive river of ice scouring out the sides and especially the floors of the valleys, making them U shaped. These primary glaciers are now largely melted but remnants like Maradalsbreen and Styggeedalsbreen remain. During

the ice ages these primary glaciers would have flowed relentlessly down until they reached the much bigger secondary glaciers. These secondary glaciers would have flowed towards the sea, creating vast steep-sided valleys as they ripped their way into the earth's surface. Utladalen and Fortunsdalen are prime examples of where these secondary glaciers once flowed. When the earth warmed up these massive secondary glaciers melted and the higher primary ones that fed them were left isolated in hanging valleys. The meltwater from the remains of the primary glaciers often plunge down the steep sides of the canyons formed by the secondary glaciers in spectacular waterfalls. Once the ice had disappeared from the canyons the rising sea filled the void and created the fjords of today. The parts of these canyons where the floor was above sea level, like Utladalen, were not flooded. They are testament to the awesome power of the melting ice and lie waiting for the next ice age to commence. Then the hanging valleys will again fill with ice and flow into these secondary larger valleys which in turn will fill with abrasive ice and flow seaward, pushing the water out of the fjords again.

CLIMATE

The climate of Hurrungane is typically maritime, and it is strongly influenced by Atlantic weather systems. West weather brings with it the associated fronts, and these are unfortunately the prevailing influence on weather in Hurrungane. However, quite frequently a high pressure system over Scandinavia or the Norwiegan/North Seas builds and this diverts the progress of the low pressures.

High pressure regularly builds in the spring and late April, and May and early June are often blessed with surperb weather. However, night temperatures frequently fall below zero in the higher valleys, especially during periods of high pressure. By the end of May the main valley floors like Ringsdalen are usually devoid of snow, but new snow can arrive at any time in May, and above 1500m any

Skagastøls ridge from Turtagrø hotel. From the left is Nordre Skagstolstind. Then Nebbet, Midtre and Vetle bunched close together, and then on the mid-right is Store Skagstølstind.

HURRUNGANE: INTRODUCTION

time in June also. Unless there has been an exceptionally heavy snowfall in the winter and spring May is the last opportunity to go ski touring or make ski ascents, and June is best avoided as it is a melting limbo-land of snow and bare patches.

The summer weather is more mixed than the usually reliable spring. However, there are at least two long periods where high pressure dominates for at least a week at a time during July and August, giving fantastic conditions in near 24 hour daylight. Temperatures during such conditions may exceed +30 celsius. However, already by the end of August a rogue front could leave some snow on the summits, although this usually melts rapidly. Summer may rarely also see some thunder storms, usually in the late afternoon and evening. A humming ice axe on the rucksack is telling you to get off the ridge pronto. If there is a westerly wind during the summer months it normally brings warmer moist air in with it. This travels along the fjord until the end of it at Fortun and Øvre Årdal when it is forced to rise, condensing rapidly into a thick mist. If during a summer visit the forecast is only of persistent fronts coming in from the west, which to be fair is not that common, it might be worth considering spending some days in north or east Jotunheimen, or even Rondane, until the weather stabilises again, which it will.

September and October can be fine months but will see the first of the winter storms and established snow on the mountains. By late October the weather deteriorates into snow storms and gales which often persist through to mid March. In addition there are very few hours of daylight. Most of the snow tends to fall towards the end of winter when the gales are diminishing. This encourages an even snow cover to become established in March for later spring ski tours. The temperature is usually -10 to -15 celsius during winter but may drop to -30 celsius during the few periods of stable high pressure.

HISTORY

People who initially settled this region were primarily hunters following the reindeer, catching them by driving them into pit traps. Eventually these hunters settled and began cultivating crops on the fertile valley floors and herding animals. During the 16th century the population increased and land became scarce. People were forced to clear remote and steep land to live on and increasingly grazed the animals in the mountain pastures in the summer. Farms like Vormeli, Avdalen and Fuglesteg were wrestled from the forest, houses were built and families moved in. The most remote was Vormeli Farm whose only link to the world was over the Keisar pass to the northwest and on to the hamlet of Fortun. If anyone died in the winter months they had to wait until the early summer to be taken to Fortun for burial. Many of these old farms, and their seters in the summer pastures, were abandoned during the course of the last 100 years. Thankfully many of these have been recently restored and are now superbly atmospheric overnighting cabins.

It was in this arena that Norwegian mountaineering or *tinderangling* flourished during the last decades of the 19th century. The birth date of *tinderangling* was probably 21 July 1876 when the much respected W.C. Slingsby made the first ascent of the most cherished Scandinavian mountain, namely Store Skagastølstind. Following this famous solo ascent an increasing number of Norwegians, notably E. Mohn, T. Heftye, T. Sulheim, O. Berge, J. Vigdal, the lady Therese Bertheau and a core of Danes, especially Carl Hall, started to climb the remaining Hurrungane mountains and peaks. In the course of the next 15 years most of them had been climbed (mostly by Carl Hall with Norwegian guides) and by the turn of the century the early pioneers of Hurrungane turned their attentions to new routes and ridge traverses, of which Hurrungane has a magnificent abundance. After that things were quiet until the 1960s when there was a Norwegian-led upsurge in climbing.

Looking up Ringsdalen in late May. The mountains are usually still plastered but the snow is almost gone from the valleys.

MASSIFS, MOUNTAIN AND PEAKS OVER 2000M IN SCANDINAVIA.

In this book I have tried to distinguish between a massif, a mountain and a peak. To distinguish between the three it is useful to rely on geographical, and in particular glacial, processes. A massif is a distinct mountainous region, often with many unifying features like geology, climate, vegetation and natural history which give it a consistent character. The mountainous massifs in Scandinavia have been separated from other massifs by an awesome glacial process over the last 50 million years. This process is the flow of secondary glaciers which have drained the upland icefields and whose abrasive power has carved deep arterial valleys into the earth's surface. These deep gashes separated the massifs once the ice had disappeared from them and now not only are obvious physical dividers but tend to act as boundaries to weather patterns, climate and natural history, encouraging us to think of each massif as a unique microcosm. Utladalen, on the east of Hurrungane, and its northwards extension Leirdalen, on the east of the Smørstabb massif, are two prime examples of these secondary glacial valleys which separate massifs and also tend to be weather divides. In mainland Scandinavia today these secondary arterial glaciers have all disappeared. Hurrungane is bordered by two such valleys.

Galhøpiggen, Scandinavia's highest mountain, lies in the Jotunheimen.

ridges while others, like Fannaråken, have none. These peaks have usually been created by glacial action on the saddles in the highest reaches of the accumulation zones of the primary glaciers, creating some smaller corries within the main corrie. Frost shattering and the erosion of bands of softer rock can also create the saddles between peaks. Usually peaks are found on the ridges leading down from the mountain. They may be very impressive and difficult to climb, like the aforementioned Skagastøls ridge peaks, or they might be dull undulations in a ridge like those on the south ridge of Bukkehø. When the actions which create peaks continue over a longer period the topography of the mountain and its ridges may change sufficiently for a deep enough saddle to create a separate mountain. This has been the case on the Styggedals ridge. Eventually, erosion of the saddles on the Skagastøls ridge will elevate these four peaks into mountains also, providing the tops remain largely unshattered by frost. Sometimes a peak on a moutain may be much harder to climb than the mountain itself, like Hettpiggen on the easy Snøhetta in Dovrefjell. The processes which create these saddles on the ridges of the mountains, like perpherial glaciation and frost shattering, may create saddles of 30m or more once they have been established a while. I therefore consider a peak to have at least 30m of ascent from the highest saddle for it to qualify as a separate peak on the mountain on which it is located. If the saddle is less than 30m I have not classified the peak at all.

Glittertind lies in the Jotunheimen ranges. It makes a magnificent ski ascent in spring.

Each massif boasts individual mountains. Frequently the mountains in a given massif are of a similar character and height. These mountains are often separated by the actions of the primary glaciers. The primary glaciers often radiate away from the centre of the massif and flow into the secondary glaciers. They gnaw into the heart of the massif, gouging out deep corries and valleys as they flowed away to meet the arterial secondary glaciers. Sometimes the headwalls of adjacent corries would be eaten away completely by the glacier to leave a pass. As they radiated away they would carve deep valleys separated by high ridges. Hurrungane is a magnificent example of this type of primary glaciation and has five superb adjacent valleys on its south east side attributable to it. This type of glaciation produced passes, deep obvious saddles and might have even split the main massif into two or three mini-massifs, as happened in Hurrungane with the Fannaråken complex to the north and the main complex to the south. The saddles produced by the general actions of this primary glaciation are generally over 100m but less than 500m. This is not only the case in Hurrungane but in most mountainous areas in Scandinavia. I therefore consider a mountain to have at least 100m of ascent from the highest saddle for it to qualify as a separate mountain.

A mountain may support a number of peaks. Some mountains, like Store Skagastølstind, may have four seperate peaks on its

This is of course a generalization, and there are some exceptions. However, it does allow us to classify all the Scandinavian 2000m tops into separate mountains and their associated peaks based on a geographical argument. A full list of all the mountains in Scandinavia which are over 2000m are given in the apendix at the end of the book. Their associated peaks are also listed. As this series of 7 books unfolds, these mountains and their associated peaks will be described as each of the regions are covered.

The Heillstugu ridge lies in the heart of the Jotunheimen ranges.

COST

One of the main concerns about a outdoor holiday in Scandinavia is the cost. Norway, and to a lesser extent Sweden, are expensive. However, with a little knowledge and planning it is possible to keep prices down. Fuel is of a comparable price. Food in the shops is only slightly more expensive but the quality of the food is of a high standard. Hotel accommodation is expensive but there are numerous cheap alternatives. Clothing and climbing equipment are expensive and it would be prudent to get it all before you go. Vices are very expensive and if you are a chain-smoking alcoholic you will embark on a financial diasaster unless take your supplies in with you. Resturants are expensive but good quality, while snack bars are expensive but poor quality. Pubs, where they exist, are expensive. Public transport is relatively cheap, very clean and extremely reliable and punctual.

Perhaps the easiest way to overcome the expenses is to go in a well stocked camper van. Offset against this are the additional expenses involved in the ferry crossing and summer restrictions imposed on camper vans on the Newcastle to Kristiansand ferry. Additionally, a campervan sometimes encourages people to be more insular and self-sufficient and mingle less with the very friendly Norwegians, most of whom speak excellent English and love to practice it. The camper van is perhaps best suited to visits of a month or more.

If a camper van is not an option then going over in a car is sensible. Again, a fair quantity of supplies can be taken. The most reasonable type of accommodation is *hytte* (huts). These are small, usually one-roomed, log cabins clustered in towns and villages throughout Scandinavia. They cost about £50 for the night and sleep four people in bunks. They have a fridge, a simple cooker, cooking utensils and a sink. Toilets and showers are usually in a shared block. It is very feasible to drive around and stop at these *hytte* when convenient each evening. If three or four are sharing they are extremely reasonable and are even good value for two people. Camping is largely free and allowed most place in Scandinavia where it does not impinge on people's privacy. Camping is discouraged near settlements and beside roads but is no problem in the wilderness.

Looking down to the Stølsmaradals ridge and into the U shaped hanging Stølsmaradalen valley from Stolsmaradalstind.

If a car or camper van is not an option then public transport is a must. This is clean and punctual and, although relatively inexpensive, the huge distances usually involved mean the cost is not insignificant. Furthermore, arrival at a bus or train station in a town will limit one's choice of accommodation. The aforementioned *hytte* may not be easily available, especially in the cities where a youth hostel or equivalent is the best option. These hostels must be prebooked. In the towns around Hurrungane like Lom, Skjolden, Øvre Årdal, Fagernes and Sogndal there are *hytte* within walking distance of the bus stop. Oslo Gardemoen airport is very well connected to trains and buses to Olso. The day and overnight trains and buses also pass

through the airport after leaving Olso on their way to the mountain regions, allowing you to be whisked off to the mountains at once. Oslo Torp airport is used by Ryanair. It is two hours south of the city, inconvient and a false enconomy to fly there. Bergen Flesland is close to the city, while Haugesund, which Ryanair use for Bergen, is over three hours away and should not be considered.

On the periphery of Hurrungane are a number of hotels, lodges and converted farms. These places provide full board and lodging for about £50 a day. They provide good value for money, a wealth of local information and weather forecasts and make a good base from which to make day trips into Hurrungane. It is also possible to leave extra stuff at these place if you are going into the interior of Hurrungane for a longer expedition. More details on these places are given in the accommodation section.

Nights out are naturally expensive in the cities. Oslo has a vibrant and thriving cafe culture, especially in the Grünerløkka area, but generally resturants are expensive and pubs are culturally bankrupt. What Oslo lacks in down to earth culture though it more than makes up for in its location, with an island peppered fjord to the south and a vast idyllic forested wilderness on its northern doorstep. Bergen is an old city and has a vibrant music scene. The pubs, especially by the Brygge, are lively and interesting and the resturants are confidently modest. The area around Bergen is also nice but the town, its people and culture are the main attractions.

FOOD AND PROVISIONS

Food and provisions can be bought in Lom, Øvre Årdal, Fagernes, Otta, Sogndal and Gaupne. In each of these small towns there is at least one supermarket, a bank autoteller for cash withdrawals and a fuel station. The supermarkets usually close at 2000hrs Monday to Friday, 1800hrs on Saturday and are closed on Sunday. The fuel stations usually close at 2200hrs seven days a week. Each of these towns, except Gaupne, also has a sports shop but the only ones to cater well for alpine sports are in Lom and in Fagernes. Camping gas is available from any of these. The sports shops close around 1700hrs Monday to Friday and midday on Saturday.

The small town of Skjolden has a shop with essential supplies only and is not open as long as the supermarkets. It would be better to continue for another 10km to Gaupne for provisions. There is a garage in the village of Fortun for fuel. This garage will also do repairs and, as parts take two days to deliver, you can leave the camper van or car and enjoy Hurrungane in the meantime. The garage may give you a lift up to Turtagro if the bus is not due.

MAPS

There is a series of 1:50,000 topographic maps which cover Norway in its entirety. This is the M711 series and is produced by Statens Kartverk, the national body. The country is divided up into squares, each of which is numbered. Each of these squares is then divided into four quadrants called I, II, III or IV respectively and is given a title name, and each one is a single map. The Hurrungane area is covered by two such maps, namely Hurrungane 1517 IV for the main southern massif and Sygnefjell 1518 III for the northern Fannaråken massif. They are made of paper and cost about £10 each.

Alternatively there is a two map 1:50,000 topographic set which is produced by Statens Kartverk in conjunction with Den Norske Turistforening. This two map set covers the entire Jotunheimen with one map covering the east, 2581 Jotunheimen Aust, and one covering the west, 2583 Jotunheimen West. Hurrungane is on the west map. The set costs about £25. This two map set is printed on plastic paper and is much more durable. It is on the 'turkart' series of maps. These are the maps I would advise getting, but the lower half of the western ridges of Austanbotntind and Soliebotntind are outside the map.

The above mentioned maps can be obtained from Stanfords in London. Tel +44 (0)20 7836 1321 or www. stanfords.co.uk. Alternatively they are available from Den Norske Turistforening in Oslo. Tel +47 2282 2800 or www. turistforeningen.no.

Finally there is a 1:25000 topographic map produced by Statens Kartverk in conjunction with Turtagrø hotel. This is printed on paper and is about £20. It is only available from Turtagrø hotel. Tel +47 5768 0800 or www.turtagro.no.

Looking up the west ridge of Sentraltind from the saddle with Vetle Skagastølstind.

FURTHER INFORMATION

There is not a lot of literature available on walking, scrambling, climbing and skiing in Hurrungane, and nothing as comprehensive as this guide. There is further information on other areas in Norway, some of which can be found in:

Tony Howard - Climbs, Scrambles and Walks in Romsdal. 2005. Printed and distributed by Cordee. Tel + 44 (0)1162543579. A thorough guidebook to the spectacular Romsdal area by Åndalsnes.

Peter Lennon - Scandinavian Mountains. 1987. Printed by West Col and distributed by Cordee. Tel + 44 (0)1162543579. Once the Bible of Scandinavian mountains, covering most areas briefly, but now dated.

Dyer, Baddeley & Robertson - Walks and Scrambles in Norway. 2005. Printed by RippingYarns.com and distributed by Cordee. Tel + 44 (0)1162543579. A book covering some 50 walks and scrambles throughout the length of Norway.

More infomation can be obtained from Den Norske Turistforening (DNT) the umbrella organisation for all the local mountain touring clubs in Norway. They own and operate hundreds of mountain lodges and huts and maintain the extensive footpath network. They will not be able to answer detailed questions about Hurrungane but can help with more general queries about Norwegian mountains, ski route markings in spring, mountain hut opening times, costs of the huts and provisions within etc. They can also help planning walking and easy scrambling itineraries and run quite a few tours in many mountain areas. They are based in Oslo. Correspondence address: Den Norske Turistforening, Postboks 7. Sentrum, 0101 Oslo, Norway. Visiting adress: Storgata 7, Oslo, Norway. Tel: +47 2282 2800. Email: info@turistforeningen.no and website: www.turistforeningen.no.

Turtagrø hotel can also provide some information about the northern side of Hurrungane. They have a web cam on their website which is very useful and also publish current and historic weather data on this website. Tel: +47 5768 0800 or www.turtagro.no.

PUBLIC TRANSPORT

Public transport in Norway consists of rail, long distance buses and local buses.

All the three main train lines connect the cities of Trondheim, Bergen and Stavanger with Oslo. There is at least one departure from each end in the morning, in the afternoon and before midnight with the journey taking 7-8 hours. On the night departures sleepers are available. The train journeys are very scenic, especially the Oslo to Bergen line. The trains operate throughout the year. Detailed times and prices, including advance booking discounts, can be obtained from NSB. Tel: +47 815 00 888 or www.nsb.no for details.

The long distance buses link most cities. These buses are very comfortable. There are departures from Oslo to Trondheim, Åndalsnes, Stryn, Årdal, Bergen and Kristiansand then Stavanger. There is normally a morning departure and late evening departure. The buses which go north to Otta stop at Oslo Gardemoen airport about 45 minutes after leaving Oslo and pick travellers up from here. The reverse is true on the return journey. It is therefore possible to land and get straight onto a mountain bound bus, arriving at Lom five hours later. There are also long distance buses from Bergen south to Stavanger and north to Årdal and Sogndal and via Stryn and Lom to Trondheim. I can only generalize about the routes here but the details of the times and prices can be found by contacting NOR-WAY bussekspress. Tel:+47 815 44 444 or www.nor-way.no. These long distance buses operate throughout the year but there may be delays in bad weather in the winter/spring due to heavy snow on the mountain sections.

The summit of Austanbotntind with its characteristic three humps is a fearful peak.

The local buses described here are from Sogndal to Lom via Turtagrø and from Turtagrø to Øvre Årdal.

The Sogndal to Otta service operates from about 20 June to 10 September. It leaves either end in the early morning and early afternoon. It stops at Lom and Turtagrø. Each of these three stages is one to one and half hours long and the total time is about four hours. The service is operated by Fjord1 Sogn Billag. For details tel: +47 5767 6600. Email: ruteopplysing.sognbillag@fjord1.no

The Øvre Årdal to Turtagrø service only operates in July and August. It leaves Øvre Årdal in the early morning, goes to Hjelle and then goes over to Turtagrø. It leaves Turtagrø mid morning, goes to Hjelle and returns to Øvre Årdal about midday. In the mid afternoon this bus also does the short trip from Øvre Årdal to Hjelle return. For further details tel:+47 5766 3010, or enquire at Turtagrø hotel. Tel +47 5768 0800.

ACCESS TO HURRUNGANE

To the north of the Hurrungane massif lies the ancient mountain route from Lom over to the inner reaches of Sognefjord at Skjolden. This important link was eventually made into a road as recently as 1938. The road, called Sognefjellsveien, is still a very important link and now provides the access to the northern parts of Hurrungane. This road, RV 55, is usually closed from late November to very late April, where drifts up to 5m are common. However, the road is usually open from Skjolden up to Turtagrø hotel throughout the year.

To the south of the massif is the industrial town of Øvre Årdal, which is sustained by a aluminium smelting works. The road from Tyinkrysset over to Øvre Årdal, the RV 53, is usually kept open throughout the winter, but during winter is closed every night and is also closed in bad weather. Øvre Årdal is usually always accessible from Lærdal, also along the road RV 53. From Øvre Årdal a minor road goes 7km up Utladalen to Hjelle. This road up to Hjelle, which is the southern gateway to Hurrungane, is open all year.

Even in early June the snow drifts beside the Sognefjell road can exceed 3m.

Between Øvre Årdal on the south and Turtagrø on the north there is a minor road which is a toll road. The toll booth lies at the halfway point. This minor road is closed all winter from late October to mid May when the deep drifts here are eventually cleared.

Further information can be obtained from the Statens vegvesen on tel:175 or from outside Norway on tel: +47 81548991. Alternatively, information on the status of the roads can be viewed on www.vegvesen.no but there is no English link.

EQUIPMENT

Ice axes are an indispensible item and as a rule of thumb should always be carried. You never know when you might need one, even in the late summer. They make glissading on steeper slopes safer and therefore more enjoyable. I prefer to use a 60-80cm shaft.

Crampons are also essential and while it may not be necessary to take them on every excursion into the mountains they should be taken on any trip which takes you over a glacier or where you may encounter steep snow or ice. The crampons do not need to be heavy 12 or 14 pointers (C2 or C3) and lightweight 10 pointers (C1) will suffice unless you are ice climbing.

Rope is needed for glacier crossings, exposed wet scrambles and climbs. Ideally one rope should cover all eventualities. I therefore find that a single 9mm rope is sufficient. This rope should be 60m to allow abseils up to 30m and also allow some extra for potential crevasse rescue. A dry proofed rope is not essential but highly recommended.

Boots should be sturdy. Four season hill walking boots with semi-stiff (B1) or preferably stiff (B2) midsoles and a supportive and durable upper are necessary. The boots should suit the crampons.

Harnesses should be lightweight and comfortable. The harness will be essential for any climbing and glacier crossings. For glacier crossings a chest harness, possibly made from a sling, is also advised.

Protection on rock is the normal choice of wedges, nuts, friends and slings. For glacier crossings ice screws are essential and either a snow anchor or stake is also advised.

Skis for hut to hut tours in the winter/spring are normally Nordic touring skis. However, for ski ascents more specialized Telemark skis, ski skins and plastic boots are more appropriate. If you want to do both then a hybrid ski, ski skins and lightweight plastic boots are sensible compromises.

Rucksacks should probably be about 40-45 litres. The rucksack should be large enough for potential rope, harness, rack, crampons, photographic equipment, food etc. If you are going to bivvy a sleeping bag, gore-tex bivvy bag and sleeping mat must also fit in.

Helmets are necessary for any ascent where there is a climb. These mountains are solid but there are sometimes scree-filled gullies and there may be scree on ledges.

Bivvy bags are advised if you are intend to bivvy on some of the ridges. A gore-tex type bivvy bag is advised. During July and early August the nights are quite short and it may be preferable to take advantage of the 20 odd hours of daylight rather than bivvy.

Sleeping bags are necessary if you intend to bivvy. During the summer a three season bag (-2 to -5 celcius) will suffice. Down is better if you are out for a single night and are confident the bivvy bag is waterproof, otherwise a synthetic one is advised, while a bit heavier it will retain some warmth if things get damp. Do not bivvy unless the forecast is good.

In the summer the melting snows fill hundreds of tumbling brooks.

CLIMBING GRADES

Throughout this book I have used two types of grades. I have graded each mountain in terms of difficulty ranging from 1 to 10. Due to the alpine nature of Hurrungane most of the mountains in the book are towards the top of the scale.

I have also graded the climbs and for this I have been consistent with the UIAA system. A brief description of both the grades I have used is given below, and these should only be used as a guide.

RATING OF ASCENT ROUTE UP MOUNTAIN		GRADE OF ROCK CLIMBING ROUTES (UIAA)	
1	A hand-in-pockets saunter in the summer over easy terrain with a marked path and no glacier crossing. Easy to ski in the winter and spring but markings covered.	I	An easy scramble with little degree of exposure. Rope is desirable but not essential.
2	An easy and relatively short ascent but the terrain may include boulders. The route may be marked. If not navigation skills are necessary.	II	A more demanding scramble sometimes with some exposure. A rope is advised especially in wet conditions. Usually ample placements for protection.
3	A straightforward ascent with rough and sometimes steep terrain, but no scrambling or glaciers. For a winter/spring ascent an ice axe and crampons are essential.	III	An easy climb with plenty of good holds. The climb may be airy and a rope is essential. Usually ample placements for protection.
4	An ascent which is generally straightforward but with some easy scrambling, but no glacier crossing. A rope is usually required for a winter/spring ascent.	IV	A climb with ample holds, but this may include some friction holds requiring balance. Often exposed but usually with ample placement for protection.
5	An intermediate ascent with difficult terrains and some easy scrambles. These ascents may involve glacier crossings. A winter/spring ascent often needs protection.	V	A demanding climb requiring a variety of techniques to utilize the holds. This grade is usually steep and exposed. Protection placement may be difficult.
6	An intermediate and long ascent with some difficult terrain and easy scrambles. These ascents may involve glacier crossings. A winter/spring ascent is quite serious.	VI	A difficult climb where training is necessary to utilize small holds and natural features. Often involves dynamic moves to attain holds. Protection may be difficult.
7	A demanding ascent with some grade II scrambles where a rope is advised. Can involve glacier crossings. A winter/spring ascent is for experienced mountaineers only.	VII	Very difficult indeed. To climb at this level requires continual training and dedication as well as inherent natural ability.
8	A difficult ascent with grade III climbing sections where rope and protection are essential. Descent often involves abseiling. In winter/spring a serious undertaking.	VIII	Extremely difficult. If you are climbing at this level Hurrungane, while having much to offer, is probably not the best playground for you.
9	Very difficult ascent with climbing to grade IV. Descent involves abseiling to reach easier terrain.	IX	Climbing at this level is the realm of elite professional climbers with sponsorship deals.
10	Very difficult and long ascents with climbing to grade IV. They have difficult escape routes should the conditions deteriorate so a good weather forecast is essential.	X	Only a handful of climbers can climb at this level.

KEY TO SYMBOLS

RATING / **2** — Rating is the difficulty of the ascent on a scale of 1 to 10. An explanation of each grade is given above.

GLACIER — Glacier indicates if there is a glacier crossing or not on the preferred ascent route.

SEASON — Season indicates which months are the most suitable for a spring ski or walking ascent, or a summer walking ascent.

CLIMBING — Climbing indicates whether there is any climbing on the preferred ascent route.

SKIING — Skiing indicates whether the ascent route is suitable for skiing in the spring months or not.

WEATHER — Some ascents can be done in wet conditions. This indicates if that is the case.

This indicates that there is no skiing, climbing or glacier crossing, or that it is not suitable for wet conditions.

This indicates that the skiing is partial or difficult. Over the weather it indicates it is possible in the wet, but not advisable.

Total distance for return trip

↕ Total ascent and descent

🕐 Total time for return journey

The final metres up the north ridge of Midtre Skagastølstind involves some scrambling.

WALKING ROUTES IN HURRUNGANE

The walking and skiing routes in Hurrungane are shown on the map inside both the back and front covers. They have been prefixed with **Hu.** or **St.** or **Ra.** which is short for Hurrungane, Stølsnos or Rauddalen respectively. After the prefix is a number 1, 2, 3. which identifies the route in that area. The number in black is the current DNT route number as given in their book "Til fots in Norge" and on their website at www.turistforeningen.no.

Most of the routes are marked with cairns and red "T" paint marks in the summer and many of these same routes are marked with large twigs pushed into the snow about every 30 yards in the late winter and spring. Some routes are not marked and DNT does not encourage some, notably **Hu.17**. The times given for the route are quite generous assuming a pack under 15kg in dry conditions, but do not take account of any rest periods or other unforeseen delays.

Hu.1 / 809	**Krossbu lodge to Skogadalsbøen lodge**	**5 hours / 15km 200m↑ / 730m↓**	**Marked in summer with cairns.**

Leave Krossbu on the west side of the Bøvre River and head south on the well marked path for 3½km to reach the top of the pass. From here there is a gradual descent down the Vetle Utledalen valley for 3km when the path from Sognefjellshytta to Skogadalsbøen (**Hu.2**) merges. Continue down the substantial, well marked track on the west side of the river for another 6km.

Here the large river Utla must be crossed on an all year bridge. After the bridge, there is a junction with one path (**Ra.1**) going upstream to Leirvassbu lodge and the other going downstream to Skogadalsbøen lodge. Take the path down the east side of the river, traversing up and down the hillside slightly through birch forests for another 2km to reach the idyllic Skogadalsbøen lodge.

Hu.2 / 810	**Sognefjellshytta lodge to Skogadalsbøen lodge**	**5 hours / 15km 50m↑ / 650m↓**	**Marked in summer with cairns. Marked in the spring with twig poles.**

From Sognefjellshytta lodge go round the west end of the lake in front of the lodge and then head south across the flat plateau. After 1½km the path to Fannaråken (**Hu.3**) forks to the south west. Continue south for another 3½km across this plateau, passing a large tarn on its east side. Soon the path makes a descent for ½km down into the valley and merges with the path from Krossbu lodge to Skogadalsbøen lodge (**Hu.1**).

This merged path is then followed for 8km to Skogadalsbøen lodge as described under **Hu.1**. In the spring the marked ski trail goes to the east end of the lake in front of Sognefjellshytta lodge and heads south east for 2km to join the route of the Krossbu Skogadalsbøen summer path which it largely follows. In the winter and spring it makes a 4km detour to the east of the Vetle Utladalen valley to avoid an avalanche prone area.

From left: Store Skagastølstind, Sentraltind, Styggedalstind and Gjertvasstind (seen from the east).

Hu.3 / 823	**Sognefjellshytta lodge to Fannaråken cabin**	**5 hours / 15km 700m↑**	**Marked in summer with cairns just to the edge of the glacier.**

Leave Sognefjellshytta lodge and head south along **Hu.2** for 1½km until a fork. Take the south west branch and round the eastern edge of Prestesteinvatnet lake. Follow the obvious path for 2km along its southern edge and then veer south along the path for a further 1km to the edge of the glacier. To proceed from here crampons, an ice axe, rope and glacial experience are necessary. Without all these it will be necessary to ask about guided trips/equipment hire from Sognefjellshytta lodge.

There are daily guided trips in July and August. The route up the glacier is steep at the start then slackens off. Beware of deep surface streams and moulins (wells) in this area. Set a course for the steep eastern slopes and gain an icy ridge. Cross to the south side of the ice ridge and head up across boulders to gain the south ridge and route **Hu.6**, and then the summit plateau. On the summit plateau head west for 1km to the cabin. For further details see 'Alternative Routes' under Fannaråken, page 41.

Hu.4 / 807	**Turtagrø hotel to Skogadalsbøen lodge**	**6 hours / 16km** **650m↑ / 750m↓**	**Marked in summer with cairns.** **Marked in the spring with twig poles.**

From Turtagrø walk up the gravel track for 4km until the fifth hairpin bend. Here the path leaves the road, heading up 300m to Ekrehytta. The path splits here with one branch **(Hu.5)** going up Fannaråken. From this split follow the lower marked path over Skrautehaugane, crossing over the river flowing out of Illvatnet lake. Continue up for 2km to Keisar pass. Descend south from the pass to Gjertvatnet and cross the river near the lake outlet.

Follow the pleasant north side of the river down for 5km into Utladalen. Here you meet the substantial Krossbu to Skogadalsbøen trail **(Hu.1)**. Cross the river Utla on a permanent bridge to gain the east side. Follow the east side of the river Utla southwards for 2km, undulating through lush birch woods to the idyllic Skogadalsbøen lodge. A marked ski trail follows a very similar route in the spring.

The summit of Austanbotntind peeks through the saddle between Store Ringstind and Soleibotntind.

The natural stone bridge over the Gjertvasselvi stream on route **Hu.15**.

Hu.5 / 820	**Turtagrø hotel to Fannaråki cabin**	**4 hours / 8km** **1200m↑**	**Marked in summer with cairns.**

From Turtagrø walk up the gravel track for 4km until the fifth hairpin bend. Here the path leaves the road, heading up 300m to Ekrehytta. Here the path splits with the lower branch **(Hu.4)** going to Skogadalsbøen lodge and the upper going up Fannaråken.

Take the upper path for three hours to reach the Fannaråken cabin. This path is steep in places, and although well marked is stony. It is not marked in winter/spring. For a full description see the preferred ascent description of Fannaråken on page 40.

Hu.6 / 808	**Fannaråki cabin to Skogadalsbøen lodge**	**4 hours / 12km** **1300m↓**	**Marked in summer with cairns.**

An obvious path leads 1km east across the summit plateau. After the east top at 1990m the path splits, with a route going north east down the side on the south ridge and then across the glacier to Sognefjellshytta **(Hu. 3)**, and a path continuing south.

Take the southern path and descend steeply down scree for an hour, descending to a saddle near a waterfall and then skirting across the mountainside until you reach the Kaiser pass. Here route **Hu. 4** is met and is then followed to Skogadalsbøen lodge.

Hu.7	**Turtagrø hotel to Skogadalsbøen lodge**	**6 hours / 16km** **650m↑ / 750m↓**	**Faintly marked in summer with cairns.**

This is an alternative route to **Hu. 4**. At hairpins on the gravel road don't head up to Ekrehytta but head south up the track for 1km to the next hairpin. Then leave the track and follow the faintly marked path east along the north of a small lake. Head south east for 1½km to enter the impressive Styggedalen valley and reach another lake. Pass to the north of this lake and

continue east for 1km to reach another lake. Pass this to the south and shortly reach another lake at 1470m. This you pass on the north and once past that lake keep north east and descend to Gjertvatnet lake on the south side of the Kaiser pass. At the south end of this lake you meet the established Turtagrø to Skogadalsbøen path which is followed as described under **Hu. 4**.

HURRUNGANE: WALKING ROUTES

Hu.8 / 821	Turtagrø hotel to Skagastølsbu shelter	3 hours / 8km 880m ⬆	Marked in summer with cairns just to the edge of the glacier.

From Turtagrø hotel cross the road and river. Follow the obvious path on the west of the river for ½km then cross the river onto the east side and ascend a steeper section. Continue up the east side for another 3km climbing steeply towards the end to reach the Tindeklubhytta cabin. Continue on the east side of the river through a boulder field while climbing up above a second and larger lake to reach the edge of the glacier. The glacier is a little more than 1km and although crevasse free does have a large bergschrund at the top which you should be wary of and is best avoided on the west side. Rope, crampons and an ice axe are necessary for the glacier. For further details see the preferred ascent description of Store Skagastølstind on page 22.

Hu.9	Turtagrø hotel up Ringsdalen	--------------	Initially well marked in summer with cairns but faint after 3km.

There is a path up Ringsdalen valley. This path is initially well marked for 3km but becomes fainter as the boulder fields are reached. This 3km section of the path is very easy and pleasant. The path eventually climbs steeply up crags on the eastern headwall of the corrie to reach the edge of the Ringsbreen glacier. From here various routes continue up each of the three Ringstinden mountains or over two saddles and down into the remoter southern valleys of Hurrungane. For further details see any of the three Ringstind descriptions on pages 36, 48 and 50 or see Route **Hu.18**.

Hu.10	Fardalen valley to Stølsmaradalen cabin	7 hours / 16km 970m⬆ / 600m⬇	Unmarked, but obvious in old drove road to summer seters and pastures.

Start in Fardalen near the small ski centre where the Åsetelvi stream comes down from the east. Climb steeply up the north side of the stream through the forest. After an ½ hour the forest thins and a collection of seter buildings appears. Cross to the south side of the stream and follow a small tributary east for 2½km through an obvious pass. Continue east for another 2½km while descending down into Gravdalen where the river Gravdøla must be waded over. On the east of the river the path forks and one path **(Hu.12)** goes down to Gravdalen and Avdalen Farm cabins. The path to Stølsmaradalen cabin climbs over a ridge and descends into another valley, Slufsedalen, where another smaller river must be waded. From here the path climbs over another ridge, Fuglenosi, and then makes a long traverse across the hillside for 2km where it meets the more distinct and marked path **Hu.13**. Follow this marked path as it traverses the hillside for another 4km to Stølsmaradalen cabin.

Hu.11/ 816	Hjelle to Avdalen Farm cabin	1½ hours / 2km 300m ⬆	Gravel track for 1km then well marked path.

Leave the car park at Hjelle and follow the farm track to Vetti Farm for 1km. Immediately after crossing the third bridge a marked track leads up the steep forested hillside for 1km on the west. After 20 minutes on this steep track the abandoned farm of Hagaberg is passed. Twenty minutes up past Hagaberg the beautiful and restored Avdalen Farm appears in a forest clearing.

There are a few old seters in the upper forests in the southern half of Hurrungane.

Goats are still milked in a few of the seters, like Avdalen Gård.

Hu.12 / 817	Avdalen Farm cabin to Fardalen valley	4½ hours / 11km 800m⬆ / 620m⬇	Unmarked route but path easily followed.

Leave Avdalen Farm and ascend steeply up for 1km to Vårstølen seter. Here to the south of the buildings the path divides to Stølsmaradalen cabin **(Hu.13)** on the north and Gravdalen cabin to the west. Take the west fork and after 1½km of easier ascent through forest Gravdalen cabin appears on the upper edge of the forest. From this cabin follow the path on the east side of the river Gravdøla for 2½km when the old drove road from Fardalen to Stølsmaradalen **(Hu.10)** is met. At this junction wade the river. From here it is 5 km over a pass to the west and down to Fardalen ski centre.

Hu.13 / 818	Avdalen Farm cabin to Stølsmaradalen cabin	3½ hours / 8km 650m ↑ / 750m ↓	Marked in summer.

Leave Avdalen Farm and ascend steeply up for 1km to Vårstølen seter. Here to the south of the buildings the path divides with a west branch going off to Gravdalen cabin (Hu.12). The main northerly branch to Stølsmaradalen continues to ascend steeply for a further hour when it levels off and emerges around the tree line. For the next 5km the path traverses along the hillside passing under some small waterfalls and crossing flower filled meadows. At the largest waterfall the old drove road from Fardalen (Hu.10) joins the path from the west and 3km after this the path from Vetti (Hu.14) joins from the south. After another pleasant 1km the bridge over the river Stølsmaradøla is reached, and the idyllic cabin is just after it in a meadow.

The continuous Styggedals ridge (left) and Skagastøls ridge (right) as seen from Galdhøpiiggen in early June. The peak in the middle behind the ridge is Store Skagastølstind.

Hu.14 / 814	Hjelle to Vetti Farm to Stølsmaradalen cabin	4½ hours / 9km 900m ↑ / 150m ↓	Gravel track for 4km then, not always obvious, marked path.

Follow the gravel track along the bottom of the gorge-like Utladalen valley crossing four bridges over the raging torrent for 5km until you come to the clearing of Vetti Farm. Follow the track up to the Farm and then descend steeply down the path on the other side of the knoll to the river again where there is a wire bridge. At the bridge a path on the east side leads north for half an hour to the bottom of Vettisfossen, the highest waterfall in Scandinavia and well worth the detour. Cross the bridge to the west side of the river Utla and start the infamous Brendeteigen ascent: 600 relentless metres, much on boulders, up the side of the gorge. Eventually, the not always obvious path levels off and after a pleasant two kilometres joins the path Hu.13. From this junction there is only a further, easy kilometre to the Stølsmaradalen cabin.

Hu.15 / 812	Skogadalsbøen lodge to Vormeli Farm	3 hours / 6 or 7km 100m ↑ / 350m ↓	Two routes, both unmarked. Possible to combine for a 6 hour circular trip.

A. Leave Skogadalsbøen and head south on the path to Vetti and Hjelle (St.1). After 2km, just after the bridge over the river Urdadøla is a fork with a path descending to the west. This unmarked path is not always obvious as it descends quickly through the lush birch forest to the river Utla. The Utla must be followed for 1km downstream before a permanent bridge is reached and it is possible to cross over to the west side. Once on the west side follow an unmarked path upstream for ½km, crossing the larger Maradøla stream on a permanent bridge to the extraordinary Vormeli Farm, which is partly restored.

B. Leave Skogadalsbøen and head north on the path to Turtagrø (Hu.4), crossing the bridge over the river Utla 2km to the north. At the junction on the west side of the bridge take the fork to Turtagrø for another ½km where there is a smaller junction and a faint fork to the south. Take this fork for ½km until you reach the Gjertvasselvi stream. Cross over a natural stone bridge. After the natural bridge the path crosses a boggy area for ½km and then meets an old drove road. The drove road is unmarked but obvious for most of the next 3½km as it traverses the birch covered hillside and descends through the abundant forest to the lonely Vormeli Farm in its fertile clearing.

Storebjørn (Big Bear) is a spectacular peak in the neighbouring Smørstabb Massif. The route to the summit goes up the demanding glacier on the ridge.

Hu.16 / 813	Vormeli Farm to Stølsmaradalen cabin	7 hours / 12km 700m↑ / 400m↓	Unmarked path, sometimes faint. This path crosses demanding terrain.

From Vormeli Farm head south along the path for ½km, over a bridge spanning the large Maradøla stream and on to the bridge over the wild river Utla. Do not cross the bridge but continue to follow the path along the west bank of the river for another 3km. During this 3km progress is slow as the path is overgrown and poorly marked. After these 3km the valley becomes even more gorge-like and the path leaves the bottom of the valley and climbs steeply up Kyrkjestigen for 300m. It is crucial to find the path up this steep slope, which might be difficult as it could be overgrown. After climbing for half an hour the path levels off and you should come across a small tarn on the south side of the

path. At this tarn the path splits with a fork going up Midtmaradalen valley to Skagastølsbu cabin, while the other branch crosses the Midtmaradøla stream (which must be waded over). Once over the stream continue up for another ½km through dense birch forest until another path is intercepted. This is the path from Stølsmaradalen cabin to Skagastølsbu cabin (**Hu.17**). This unmarked path is more obvious. Follow it south west up for a steep ½km until it levels out and goes through a saddle between the main mountain and a pronounced knoll called Snørestødet. From here it is an easier 2km descent on a more obvious path to the delightful Stølsmaradalen cabin.

	Stølsmaradalen cabin to Skagastølsbu shelter	7 hours / 12km 1130m ı / 220m▼	Unmarked path, suitable only for experienced mountaineers.

Leave Stølsmaradalen cabin and head 2km north east climbing up to the pass by Snørestødet. From here the path continues north east, but descends for 1km. As the tree line approaches at the bottom of a steeper descent, the path forks, with one branch continuing the descent down to Vormeli Farm (**Hu.16**). Do not take this descending fork, but take the fork which makes a level traverse north west into the Midtmaradalen valley. Wade the stream to gain the north side of this perfectly formed U-shaped glacial valley. Follow the north side of the stream for 7km passing up through wonderful meadows under huge impressive walls

and peaks. The landscape here is truly exceptional. As the end of the valley approaches a steep headwall appears. The way up this headwall is difficult and a rope could be useful for added security. Initially head towards the summit of Store Skagastølstinden until you reach an altitude of 1400m. Then bear due west and scramble up a scree covered rake, often with a snowfield to traverse, to a small gap between the cliffs. From the top of this gap there is a further 1km to ascend across scree, slabs and some snowfields to Skagastølsbu cabin. From here it is another three hours to Turtagrø hotel (see route **Hu.8**).

Hu.18 / 822	Turtagrø hotel to Stølmaradalen cabin	11 hours / 24km 1140m↑ /1140m↓	Route across glaciers. Suitable for experienced mountaineers only.

Leave Turtagrø hotel and walk along the road to Øvre Årdal for 2km and then take the path up Ringsdalen valley (**Hu.9**). Follow the good path up the valley floor on the east side of the stream for 3km, and then continue for another 1km across boulders to a small lake. From the lake pick a way through the moraine in the direction of Midtre Ringstinden for 1km. Then start to ascend the steeper scree slope on the east to reach a snowfield under a

rock band. Climb the snowfield and scramble up through the rock band to gain a flatter moraine area which is followed south east for ½km to the edge of the glacier. This is a crevassed glacier and crampons, an ice axe, rope and experience are essential. Ascend the glacier for 1km in a southerly direction to reach the Ringsskard pass. See the Østre Ringstind, page 50, for further details. From Ringsskard pass continue south onto the larger

Stølsmaradalsbreen glacier and cross it in a south direction for 2½km, keeping close under the impressive spire of Stølsmaradalstinden to reach its south ridge. Leave the glacier here and climb a knoll (1787m) to the south. Descend this knoll to the southern saddle and then cross the glacier to the east in a due east direction for 1km. From the east side of this glacier a line of cairns follows the crest of a 4km undulating ridge

to the south east. Follow this pleasant ridge and after passing well to the north of a tarn begin a poorly marked steep descent down the hillside, keeping on the north side of a growing stream. At the bottom of this steep slope the path from Avdalen Farm to Stølsmaradalen cabin (Hu.13) is met. It is only 1km to the latter. For more details on the descent from Stølsmaradalsbreen glacier see the Stølsmaradalstind 'Alternative Routes' on page 45.

Saksi also lies in the neighbouring Smørstabb massif. The easiest route to the summit goes up the north (right) ridge after a substantial glacier crossing.

St.1 / 811	Hjelle to Skogadalsbøen lodge via Vetti Farm and Ingerdbu cabin	7 hours / 18km 1240m ↑ / 510m ↓	Marked in summer with cairns.

Leave Hjelle and follow the 5km track to Vetti. Here leave route **Hu.14** and start to follow the steep marked track up through the forest for nearly an hour until the path forks. The north east fork skirts the top of the spectacular Vettisfossen and is worth taking for the long kilometre to the idyllic Vetismorki meadows and seters. The new Ingerdbu cabin is here. From here the path heads north east across the meadow and into the forest, crossing marshy terrain for 2km until it crosses the foot bridge over the Fleskadøla stream. The path then climbs through the forest for another 1km before emerging onto a plateau to the west of the

now tranquil Fleskadøla stream. On the bank opposite two seter buildings the path forks. Take the west fork and climb the ridge for 2km, with stunning views to Hurrungane. At the top of the climb the path skirts across the west side of Friken for 3km before it descends back into the forest high above Vormeli Farm, before shortly crossing the Urdadøla stream. From this permanant bridge the path continues north for 1km until a fork on the east to Tyin. Ignore it and continue north for another ½km on the path through the woods to cross the Skogadøla stream and Skogadalsbøen lodge just beyond.

Ra.1 / 806	Leirvassbu lodge to Skogadalsbøen lodge	6 hours / 20km 610m ↑ / 40m ↓	Marked in summer with cairns. Marked in spring with twig poles.

From Leirvassbu lodge head south on the track that crosses the outflow from the lake. It is easiest to continue on this track rather than follow the path which crosses the track several times as it heads down Gravdalen. However, the track goes round the south of the Gravdalsdammen lake and stops while the path goes to the north of it and continues down the valley. So before the lake, and definitely before the track crosses a bridge, leave the track and head north for a few hundred metres to intercept the path. On the north side of the lake cross the Sandelvi stream by footbridge and continue to the dam. From this dam follow the footpath down the valley on the north side of the youthful Utla river for 4km until it crosses onto the south side over a permanent bridge. On the south side of the bridge there is a fork heading up to Olavsbu cabin some 11km away and the fork to

take heading down to Skogadalsbøen lodge some 7km away. These pleasant, easy 7km take you down the south side of the river Utla towards the spectacular vista of Hurrungane. About half way down, by the tree line, 2 other valleys converge to form the upper end of the 30km canyon which is Utladalen. The path veers south as you enter the trees and keeps on the east side of the river, passing a bridge to Turtagrø. From this bridge the path continues for 2km through lush fertile woodland to reach Skogadalsbøen lodge. In the spring the marked ski route almost follows this path. However, as it approaches the converging valleys at the bottom of Storutladalen it veers north west over the knoll of Tungehaugane to avoid avalanche prone slopes. This detour intercepts the Krossbu to Skogadalsbøen ski track (Hu.1) and is followed for 4km south to Skogalsdalsbøen lodge.

ACCOMMODATION IN HURRUNGANE

Accommodation in and around Hurrungane is plentiful. On the north side of the massif beside the road Rv 55 there are two lodges and a hotel. On the south side of the massif there are hotels in Årdalstangen and Øvre Årdal, a campsite with hytte and a short walk from Hjelle is the restored Avdalen Farm. In the interior of Hurrungane there are a number of cabins and a lodge. The cabins are rudimentary and provisions must be taken in. These cabins are usually locked with a standard DNT key and these are available to all DNT members for a small deposit. For details of becoming a member of the DNT contact the DNT. Tel +47 2282 2800 or www. turistforeningen.no.

The management, cost, opening times etc. of all the accommodation is liable to change from year to year and it is important to check before setting off. For locations of this accommodation refer to the map inside the front or back covers.

Hotel or lodge with all facilities.	Private	DNT-Owned	
Cabin with self-service facilities and provisions.	Private	DNT-Owned	
Cabin with no facilities or provisions.	Private	DNT-Owned	

KROSSBU

www. krossbu.no
Tel: +47 61 21 29 22

A charming private old lodge, now over 100 years old, which lies beside the Sognefjellet road at 1270m. It is an excellent spot to explore the Smørstabb massif and gives good access to the north eastern areas of Hurrungane. It is relatively cheap. During May and in the summer months there are guided trips from here over the glacier to Leirvassbu. If anything negative can be said about Krossbu lodge, and it is hardly fair to do so as it is otherwise so comfortable, it is that there are often parties of elder schoolchildren here doing various outdoor courses. Krossbu lodge is usually open during the Easter weeks and all the weekends in May. It then opens fully from early June to the end of September.

SOGNEFJELLSHYTTA

www.sognefjellet.no
Tel: +47 61 21 29 34

A private lodge which lies on the highest point of the Sognefjellet road at 1410m. It is a comfortable atmospheric lodge with good food. It is the best place to access Skogadalsbøen lodge. In the summer there is daily guiding from the lodge across the Fannaråkbreen glacier to the summit of Fannaråken (which is the most interesting ascent route). It is open during the Easter weeks and then from early May until late September.

TURTAGRØ HOTEL

www. turtagro.no
Tel: +47 57 68 08 00

The cradle of climbing in Hurrungane. The hotel is well over 100 years old and now on its second reincarnation, after the first was totally destroyed by fire in 2001. It was here that the great pioneers of Norwegian mountaineering set off on famous trips. A visit to the hotel illustrates the 125 year relationship between the four generations of the Berge/Drægni family and generations of visiting mountaineers. The hotel is very comfortable but expensive. However, it also provides some basic cheap accommodation in an annex and this, together with its library of mountaineering books and friendly atmosphere, makes it a very attractive base. The hotel has a long history of arranging guided ascents which continues today. There are plenty of good campsites across the river Berg and in many other areas in the vicinity also. Turtagrø is located on the north side of the main massif and is a great starting point for most of the mountains over 2000m. The hotel is usually open from just before Easter until early October.

FANNARÅKEN CABIN

http://home.no.net/fanaraak/
Tel:+47 48 15 22 44 or DNT Tel:+47 22 82 28 00

This cabin is run by DNT. It is the highest cabin in Scandinavia at an altitude of 2068m! Built in 1926 and 1934, one of the two cabins was a weather station but is now also a hill walker's cabin. Due to its absolutely stunning location, the views from here are probably the best from any window in Europe. Despite the wild location of the cabin it is extremely comfortable. The cabin is only open during the summer months from late June/early July to late August/late September. During the rest of the year it is hermetically sealed and no access is possible. There are daily guided trips from here down across the glacier towards Sognefjellshytta lodge.

SKOGADALSBØEN LODGE

www.skogadalsboen.com
Tel: +47 97 56 90 94

One of DNT's flagship lodges. Well sited on a flat clearing in the birch forest overlooking Utladalen and Hurrungane, it is at the hub of a web of walking tracks in the summer and skiing trails in the spring. It is a large traditional lodge but has all the modern comforts. During the Easter period and from late June to late September it is staffed and offers refreshments, meals and accommodation. The prices are the DNT standard prices. From mid October to mid February it is completely closed. However, outside the above times there is a self-service accommodation facility with provisions available, again all at the standard DNT prices. The lodge is extremely well run privately on behalf of DNT and they have produced a very comprehensive website with loads of excellent information, including prices, and in English.

SKAGASTØLSBU SHELTER

Also better know as the "Hytta på Bandet", Skagastølsbu has been providing shelter for mountaineers in Hurrungane since 1894. It was a self-service cabin with facilities; however, due to overuse, abuse of the honesty system and differing interpretations of legislation preventing any commercial activity in national parks, DNT, who run the cabin decided to remove the equipment and facilities and relegate the cabin's status to an emergency shelter only. As a consequence the stone shelter is damp, dirty and threadbare and no longer the cosy cabin it once was, but will do when the going gets tough.

UTLADALEN CAMPING

Tel: +47 57 66 34 44

This is a campsite just south of Hjelle by Øvre Årdal. It also has a selection of huts for hire on a nightly basis, with four beds and cooking facilities in each, at very reasonable prices. It is a great place to prepare for a trip into southern Hurrungane as there is a nearby supermarket in Øvre Årdal, but is not the sort of place to linger as there are the wonderful alternatives further up the valley.

AVDALEN FARM CABIN

www. ardalturlag.no
Tel: +47 57 72 06 14

This is an old farm in a dramatic setting on a small plateau overlooking Utladalen. It was abandoned but has been beautifully restored in the last 20 years and is now run as a farm again in the summer months. Most of the farming activity centres on maintaining the meadows and looking after grazing animals, mostly goats. The Farm accommodates passing walkers with refreshments and also provides very reasonably priced meals and accommodation. It is open from late June to mid September. Outwith this period there is self-service accommodation with a key. It is not known whether this is the standard DNT key or not.

Skogadalsbøen lodge is a comfortable hub on the path network in east Hurrungane.

GRAVDALEN CABIN

www. ardalturlag.no
Tel: +47 57 72 06 14

The old summer seter for Avdalen Farm. It is only has two beds. It is self-service and locked. It is not known if this key is the standard DNT key or not, and it is best to check with Avdalen Farm anyway. The cost will be exactly as, or similar to, the standard DNT prices for self-service cabins. It is run by Årdal Turlag.

STØLSMARADALEN CABIN

www. turistforeningen.no
DNT Tel: +47 22 82 28 00

A hidden gem. It is probably the most charming of all the DNT cabins and retains much of its old seter atmosphere. It is superbly sited at the lip of a meadow overlooking Utladalen and Vettisfossen. It has only four beds and gas for cooking but no provisions. It is locked with the standard DNT key and is available from mid February to mid October. Outwith these dates there is no access. The cost is the very reasonable DNT standard price for self-service cabins.

VETTI FARM CABIN

Tel: +47 57 66 30 24

Used to provide accommodation and may well do so again in the near future. At the moment it just provides refreshment and meals. It is 30 minutes' walk from here to the highest waterfall in northern Europe, Vettisfossen.

INGJERDBU CABIN

Tel: +47 57 66 30 24

Burnt down in June 2001 but has since been rebuilt. It is situated beside a collection of old seter buildings on a high forested plateau above the Vettisfossen waterfall. It is an extremely idyllic setting. The cabin is self-service only and is accessed with the DNT standard key. It is only available between early July to mid September. It is an hour's walk from Vetti Farm. The cabin is run by Sogn og Fjordane Turlag. The prices are the standard DNT prices, which are good value.

VORMELI FARM CABIN

A remarkable restored farm deep in the lush fertile depths of Utladalen. The Farm was in use for 250 years, which is incredible considering its isolation. So remote was the Farm that the only contact with the outside world was over the Kaiser pass to the north then down to Fortun, and this was only possible in the summer months. It was abandoned as a farm in 1867 and was then used as a seter for Fortun farmers until 1946 when it was totally abandoned. On July 21 1876 it was the starting point for the most significant day in Norwegian mountaineering when Slingsby, Mohn and Lykken set off from here to climb Store Skagastølstind. The seter was a favourite place for Slingsby. In 1975 a group, "Vormelis venner", organised the restoration of the main building with some support from the DNT. It is now possible to overnight in the main building, but there are no provisions or bedding and it is locked with the standard DNT key. The cost is the very reasonable DNT standard price for self-service cabins.

The idyllic Stolsmaradalen cabin lies in an alpine meadow beneath high glaciated peaks.

1.1 STORE SKAGASTØLSTIND or STOREN

The towering summit of Store Skagastølstind and the steep south face looks a daunting prospect from the south. To the right of the picture is the top section of the Slingsbybreen glacier which leads up to Mohns skard. The peak on the very right is Vetle Skagastolstind.

Store Skagastølstind, 2405m, otherwise known as "Storen", is the jewel in the crown of Scandinavian mountains. Its first ascent in 1876 symbolized the start of mountaineering in Norway. It is a magnificent tower of hard gabbro on an outlying spur from the main ridge, separated by Mohns skard saddle.

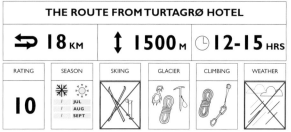

THE ROUTE FROM TURTAGRØ HOTEL

⇄ **18** KM ↕ **1500** M 🕐 **12-15** HRS

RATING	SEASON	SKIING	GLACIER	CLIMBING	WEATHER
10	JUL / AUG / SEPT				

From Turtagrø hotel cross the bridge and follow the path on the west side of a small river. After 1km the path crosses to the east of the river and rises to gain another flat stretch which is 3km long. At the end of this flat stretch the path rises again and zigzags up the valley side for 100m in height. At the top of this rise you will reach Heimste Skardstølsvatnet lake and the Norwegian Tindeklubbhytta Hut. Continue to Fremste Skardstølsvatnet lake and follow the path initially along the shore before climbing up to the glacier. Do not be tempted into climbing too early as you will be led into a boulder field.

Once on the glacier don crampons and rope up, then head straight across the glacier to the saddle. This glacier is usually problem free except for one large bergschrund at the top, just before the saddle. This bergschrund is best passed slightly to the west side of the saddle, where it might not exist and there is a far gentler gradient. Just beyond and to the east of the saddle is the Skagastølsbu shelter, known as "Hytte på Bandet". This shelter is 3 hours from Turtagrø.

From Skagastølsbu shelter Storen looks especially daunting but upon starting unfolds into a sustained scramble. On leaving the cabin you must head well out onto the south face to avoid a

steeper area of more slippery slabs. There is a multitude of cairns marking a plethora of routes. The preferred route is to go well out onto the south face climbing slowly and traversing across the south face for ½km until a large steep snowfield is reached. It is safest to traverse right across this snowfield rather than climb it. Once across the snowfield head directly up across scree and rough-textured gabbro slabs.

After at least one and a half hours of sustained scrambling you will arrive at a steeper section of slabs. There are two routes, one up a small gully that turns into 45 degree slabs, and the preferred route which is 20m to the left (west) starting from a ledge slightly higher up. The latter route follows a 50 degree slab up a narrowing crack for 8m and then continues up an easier slab on the left of a large block to bring you up to a shelf where scrambling can start again. The slabs are grade III. A rope is recommended as the consequences of a slip here are dire.

From the top of these slabs there is an obvious route up and across the south face to the south east ridge and the Hjørnet. There is a distinct bump in the ridge about level with the top of these slabs but this is much lower down and is called Det Falske Hjørnet. The real Hjørnet is a good 150m above this and not so pronounced. It is the higher one to aim for. For the last 40m the route up to the Hjørnet follows a comfortable gully. At the Hjørnet the climbing begins. It is two full pitches followed by a 20m pitch. This is also the bottom of the 55m abseil from just below the summit. Depending how busy the route is it will take a minimum of two hours to return to this spot, so it is best to don all necessary clothing and leave rucksacks here as Heftyes' renne is quite narrow.

From the Hjørnet the route now follows a ledge heading north east above the Slingsbybreen glacier. Initially the ledge is narrow but

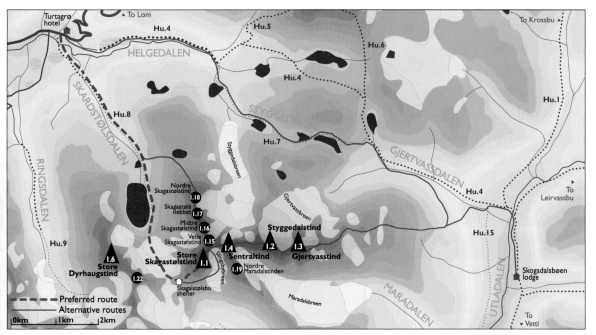

as the traverse continues to the midpoint it widens considerably. At the midpoint a small ridge is climbed to gain a grade II slab. This slab leads to a another shelf from which a grade III slab rises for 6m at the far end. At the top of this grade III slab is an excellent belay point on a large and secure shelf.

The second pitch is Heftyes' renne itself. The crux of the whole climb is getting off the shelf and into the chimney, a mere 4m of grade V climbing. Once in the narrow chimney the climbing is initially grade IV but soon reverts to grade III as it widens. After 25m the chimney opens up and soon disappears entirely. There is a further 25m to scramble up to reach another belay point on a little top just under the main summit. From the top of this second pitch on the small top there is a little chasm to cross then a grade II slab for 20m to the summit itself of the most coveted mountain in Scandinavia.

The descent is back to the little summit, 20m to the south, crossing the chasm again to the belay point. From here it continues for 15m back down towards Heftyes' renne until you pass a large rock on the right (south). Veer right (south) under this block and continue to scramble down, veering right again (south west) for a further 15m until you reach another large rock at the top of the 55m vertical abseil down a right angled corner. At the top of the abseil is a large rock which makes an excellent anchor. The 55m abseil is initially slightly overhanging, but soon becomes vertical for 35m. The last 15m are a jumble of slabs in a gully until you reach the flatter area by the Hjørnet.

From here it is a quick 20-30 minute descent across the south face to the top of the slabs that saw the day's first climbing. These 45 degree slabs should also now be abseiled. Instead of continuing to the point that you climbed up previously it is suffice to stop 20m before, and using the excellent anchor point abseil the 55m down the 45 degree slabs and the gully at the bottom to reach the scree again. From the top of the scree it is quite straightforward to return to the Skagastølsbu shelter by retracing you steps. However, it is difficult to resist the instinct to head straight down, but you must continually veer to the east and keep well away from the ridge to avoid the slippery slabs further down. Once at the Skagastølsbu cabin there are still two and a half hours to go to Turtagrø across the glacier and down the valley.

Store Skagastølstind looks especially daunting from Midtre Skagastølstind.

Alternative Routes

There are now many routes to the summit, some of exceptional quality, but all require climbing. The original route, Slingsby's route, is now seldom used because the glacier, Slingsbybreen, can cause difficulties. The easiest route via Andrews' renne is grade IV; however, there is a danger of stone and rock fall from the scree filled gully above. The most popular route is the one described above, namely Heftyes' renne, which is a grade V for the 4m crux and otherwise offers some marvellous grade III climbing for its two rope lengths. The only drawback is that as the season is short the route might be busy during periods of settled weather during late July to early August. The most common descent is the 55m abseil described above which ends back just above the Hjørnet, which is where the Heftyes' renne route starts.

1.1 STORE SKAGASTØLSTIND or STOREN

Store Skagastølstind from Sentraltind to the east. On the very bottom left is the "Falsk Hjørnet". Above this is the real Hjørnet from where the shelves lead round to Heftyes' renne gully. On the right side of the picture is Mohns skard saddle at the top of Slingsbybreen glacier.

The original route, Slingsby's route, goes up from Turtagrø to Skagastølsbu shelter. From here it follows the 1km shelf called Berges chausée, under the south face to Slingsbybreen glacier. The route then climbs the very variable glacier to Mohns skard saddle, as described on the Sentraltind preferred route, page 30. From Mohns skard the route climbs up the north east ridge, with a pitch of grade III, to the summit as described below in the Skagastøls ridge traverse description.

A classic, but much more demanding ascent is via the entire Skagastøls ridge. This again starts from Turtagrø hotel and goes over the peaks of Nordre Skagastølstind, Skagastølsnebbet, Midtre Skagastølstind and Vetle Skagastølstind before reaching Mohns skard and then climbing up the north east ridge of Storen. Follow the route **Hu.8** up Skardstølsdalen to the Tindeklubhytta cabin as described in the preferred section below. Once at this cabin leave the track and head up the side valley to the east. The grass slopes soon give way to stones as you ascend towards a saddle with a lake at 1584m. Before you reach the west end of the lake leave this stony valley and start to clamber up the ridge to the south east. This relentless ridge ascends over 600m quite steeply up unpleasant boulder fields to the top of Nordre Skagastølstind. From here there is initially a steep descent to the south towards Nebbskar, the saddle with Skagastølsnebbet, but this soon eases off, and the ascent up to Skagastølsnebbet is quite straightforward with a couple of sections of easy scrambling towards the top. From the top of Skagastølsnebbet however the going gets more serious. Initially there is a steep 30m scramble down into a deep notch called V-skaret. From the bottom of V-skaret there is a 40m two pitch climb to ascend the south side of this gash. The lower pitch is 20m and is a grade IV climb while the upper pitch is 20m exposed grade III. There is a good stance between the pitches. At the top of this climb there are some shallow slabs which lead to a small flat area called Berges stol. From Berges stol the arête narrows and steeply rises for another 30m of grade III climbing to the exposed top of Midtre Skagastølstind.

After Midtre Skagastølstind the arête continues south to Vetle Skagastølstind. This section, which is arguably the finest of the whole traverse, begins with a short exposed descent down the arête until it levels off after 25m. Then comes a tricky down climb which is a good grade III for 10m and where most people will feel more comfortable abseiling. After the abseil the arête becomes even sharper and narrower and it is necessary to creep along one very thin 10m section before it broadens out again. From this narrowest section the arête is largely horizontal for 300 interesting metres to the foot of Halls hammer. During this level section there are a number of short interesting scrambles to overcome to reach Halls hammer. Halls hammer itself is a vertical 15m crag with two vertical cracks, each of which are grade VII. However, the ascent of it can be avoided by making a short detour to

the east of the crag and crossing a slab called Patchells sva. After Patchells sva there is a short boulder filled corner which climbs for 10m to gain the arête again, just above Halls hammer. This detour is grade IV. From the top of Halls hammer the arête continues south but now starts to climb up to Vetle Skagastølstind, where there are again numerous short grade III scrambles.

From Vetle Skagastølstind there is a choice of either descending the south ridge to Mohns skard or descending the east ridge to the saddle with Sentraltind and then clambering across self formations on the south face of Vetle Skagastølstind to Mohns skard. The south ridge is shorter but involves two 25m abseils down its steep apex. If coming the other way the south ridge of Vetle Skagastølstind is grade IV for a lower pitch and grade V for the upper pitch before the top. The east ridge is relatively easy with some

The difficult obstacle of Halls hammar has to be climbed if going north to south.

short scrambling sections down to the saddle. From here it can be difficult to find the right place to begin the traverse across the south face of Vetle Skagastølstind, as the shelf formations are not so obvious here. In addition to this there could be some lingering snow patches, which are often icy. The best place to start the traverse is at the lowest point of the saddle but it is only after 50m of traversing across a grade III scramble that the shelves becomes more obvious. As you approach Mohns skard the shelves become wide and easy.

From Mohns skard the final hurdle of the north east ridge of Storen has to be overcome. This was also Slingsby's task late in the evening on 21 July 1976, when he made the first ascent, and he had to do it solo while his two companions waited at the saddle. Initially the route goes up the arête and then veers to the west side of it for a grade III section about half way up after 100m, which most choose to abseil if descending. From this point the route now regains the crest and continues up it veering slightly to the east side

before reaching the false summit called Slingsbys' fortopp, where there is a short airy walk across the roof of Hurrungane to the main summit. The total time from Turtagrø to the summit is about 9-14 hours.

The return can either be by the descent route given in the preferred section involving the 55m abseil to the Hjørnet and then to Skagastølsbu shelter and Turtagrø, or back to Mohns skard and down Slingsbybreen to Skagastølsbu shelter and Turtagrø as described on the Sentraltind pages (30-31). Either descent is likely to take an additional 5-7 hours. Alternatively, it is possible to return to Mohns skard and then continue along Styggedals ridge to Gjertvasstind and Skogadalsbøen lodge but this will take 9-14 hours and will probably necessitate a night's bivouac on the ridge. If doing this greater traverse it is normal to do it the other way round from east to west, doing the Styggedals ridge first and then descending the Skagastøls ridge on the second day. For further details on this greater traverse see the Sentraltind, Styggedalstind and Gjertvasstind pages (26-31).

Peaks associated with Store Skagastølstind

The Skagastøls ridge from the west. From the left is Nordre Skagastølstind, Skagastølsnebbet, the notch of V-skaret, Midtre Skagastølstind, the step of Halls hammer, then Vetle Skagastølstind followed by Mohns skard saddle and Store Skagastølstind.

1.15 Vetle Skagastølstind

Vetle Skagastølstind, 2340m, lies at the southern end of the Skagastøls ridge. It is usually climbed in conjunction with a traverse of the Skagastøls ridge from Storen to Nordre Skagastølstind or vice versa. It is sometimes climbed as part of the classic two day Styggedals/Skagastøls ridge traverse. There are three ridges that lead up to its summit.

The south ridge from Mohns skard is steep and involves two 25m pitches, the lower at grade IV and the upper at grade V. About one hour

The north ridge from the saddle with Midtre Skagastølstind begins with the infamous obstacle of Halls hammer, a 15m grade VII crack. This crack can be avoided on the east side with a grade IV slab, Patchells sva. After Halls hammer the north arête continues to the summit with many scrambling sections, all of grade III. About one hour

The east ridge from the saddle with Sentraltind is quite straightforward, and although relatively exposed only involves easy scrambling. About half an hour

To reach any of the three saddles is itself a difficult task and is described in the Storen alternative routes section above or on the Sentraltind page (30-31).

1.16 Midtre Skagastølstind

Midtre Skagastølstind, 2284m, lies in the middle of the Skagastøls ridge. It is usually climbed in conjunction with a traverse of the Skagastøls ridge from Storen to Nordre Skagastølstind or vice versa. It is sometimes also climbed as part of the classic two day Styggedals/Skagastøls ridge traverse. There are two ridges that lead up to its summit.

The north ridge from V-skaret is steep and involves three pitches. The first two 20m pitches from V-skaret's depths are grade IV then grade III. These lead to a flat area called Berges stol. From Berges stol there is another 30m grade II pitch to the top. About one hour.

The south ridge from the saddle with Vetle Skagastølstind is exposed and dramatic. From the foot of Halls hammer the arête stretching northwards is largely level for 300m but contains many interesting scrambling sections. At the end of this level section the arête narrows yet further and is very airy for a 10m section, where it is necessary to creep along. At the end of this exposed 10m section there is a small notch. On the south side of this notch is an exposed 10m grade III climb, which leads onto the arête again. From the top of this climb there is a short 25m scramble to the top. About one hour.

To reach the bottom of V-Skaret from the north involves a long grind up Nordre Skagastølstind and then an easy scramble from here over to Skagastølsnebbet and a short easy scramble down to V-skaret's depths. To reach the saddle on the north side involves extensive climbing as described above in the Storen alternative routes section or on the Sentraltind page (30-31).

1.17 Skagastølsnebbet

Skagastølsnebbet, 2222m, lies towards the northern end of the Skagastøls ridge. It can be climbed on its own from Turtagrø without major problems and is also sometimes climbed in conjunction with a traverse of the Skagastøls ridge from Storen to Nordre Skagastølstind or vice versa.

The south ridge is a short 35m scramble up from the bottom of V-skaret to the summit on the south side of the peak. This takes quarter of an hour.

From the north there is a problem free walk up from the saddle, Nebbskar, with Nordre Skagastølstind involving just one easy short scramble. From Nebbskar to the top it is half an hour.

See the Storen alternative routes section above for more details.

1.18 Nordre Skagastølstind

Nordre Skagastølstind, 2167m, lies at the northern end of the Skagastøls ridge. It is commonly climbed on its own from Turtagrø, and sometimes in conjunction with a traverse of the Skagastøls ridge.

The south ridge from the Nebbskar saddle with Skagastølsnebbet is an interesting walk which steepens slightly towards the top, where some easy scrambling is necessary. From the saddle to the summit it is a short half an hour hour.

From the north, Nordre Skagastølstind can be climbed from Turtagrø hotel. The route goes up Skardstølsdalen for 4km to the Tindeklubbhytta cabin. From here it ascends the side valley to the lake at 1584m before going up the relentless boulders of the north east ridge for 600m. From Turtagrø to the top is about four to five hours with about three hours' return.

See the Storen alternative routes section above for more details.

1.2 STYGGEDALSTIND

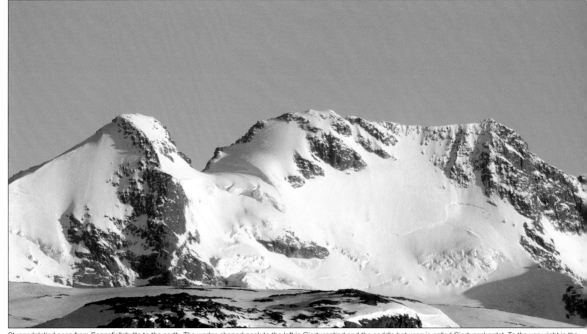

Styggedalstind seen from Sognefjellshytta to the north. The wedge shaped peak to the left is Gjertvasstind and the saddle between is called Gjertvasskardet. To the very right is the saddle with Sentraltind.

Styggedalstind, 2387m, is the fourth highest mountain in Scandinavia. It dominates the eastern half of the classic view of Hurrungane found on so many calendars. It comprises two tops, the higher eastern and slightly lower western, which are connected by a horizontal but jagged arête.

THE ROUTE FROM SKOGADALSBØEN LODGE

⇌ **20** KM   ↕ **1750** M   ⏱ **13-16** HRS

RATING	SEASON	SKIING	GLACIER	CLIMBING	WEATHER
10	❄ ☀ / JUL / AUG / SEPT	✕			✕

Climb Gjertvasstind as described on the Gjertvasstind page(28-29). From that summit make the difficult descent down the 120m to the saddle called Gjertvasskardet, probably across some ice patches. This descent is also described on those pages. Once at the saddle you can start to ascend the east ridge of Store Styggedalstind.

From the saddle continue up the glacier for 15m and then cross onto the rock ridge. Be wary of a small bergschrund here. Continue up the rock ridge along the south edge of the glacier. Initially this rock ridge is moderately steep for 40m but the scrambling is easy. Then the ridge steepens considerably for 15m and the scrambling is grade III. If wet it is wise to use rope here.

After this steeper 15m section the gradient of the ridge eases considerably but the scrambling continues to be interesting on firm rock, with the odd section at grade II. Occasionally it might be easier, but not necessary, to venture onto the snow or glacier on the north side to bypass a more difficult section. After a short hour's scrambling from the saddle the summit is reached.

To return follow the ascent route down to the saddle and then over Gjertvasstind again. In the event of the weather deteriorating

badly this is still the preferred escape route. The descent down Gjertvassbreen glacier from Gjertvasskardet is riddled with crevasses, initially steep and could be avalanche prone in certain conditions. This glacier descent demands considerable mountaineering expertise.

To continue to west top follow the ridge westwards for a short half hour along the sensational arête with the occasional scramble and downclimb, all short but some tricky, especially in the wet. From the west top it is possible to descend to the saddle between Styggedalstind and Sentraltind by reversing the ascent route described in the alternative section below.

Alternative Routes

Store Styggedalstind can be climbed from the east or the west. Both routes are demanding in terms of time and involve climbing techniques. Of these two routes the one from the east over Gjertvasstind is probably the least difficult and not as long; however, it usually requires ice climbing techniques. This is the route I have described above. The other route from Sentraltind I describe here. There are other routes up the north face but these are much more serious and outwith the scope of the book.

From the saddle between Sentraltind and Styggedalstind (which is not easy to gain from Sentraltind as it involves four abseils) the west ridge of Styggedalstind looms large. Initially the arête at the foot of Sentraltind is level but narrow. Follow this east for 300m until a tower which involves a tricky 5m grade III scramble to overcome. Once on the short easy west side of the tower the arête is again level but now about 4m wide for another 150m until you reach the bottom of the west ridge proper of Styggedalstind.

At the bottom of the west ridge is a level bivouac site big enough for three people end to end; Hotel Stygg. This site is exposed to southern weather.

1.2 STYGGEDALSTIND

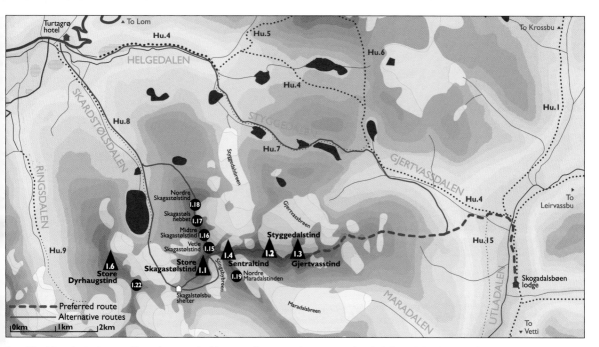

From Hotel Stygg begin the scramble up the west ridge. This is initially up an easy shallow arête but soon this becomes very steep and it is necessary to traverse out to the south side here. On this south side there is a broad gully which has to be climbed. This is a difficult grade III for about 20m and a rope is wise in the wet. If descending this section an abseil may be preferable to a downclimb. At the top of this gully you will be back on the apex of the ridge where there is a further 40m of easy scrambling to the west top. From the west top to the main top there is a sensational half hour's walk along the highest arête in Scandinavia with a few short, and occasionally tricky, scrambles and downclimbs.

It is quite usual to climb Styggedalstind as part of the classic traverse from Skogadalsbøen lodge to Turtagrø over both Styggedals ridge and Skagastøls ridge, which takes two days and a night's bivouac. Potential bivouac sites are Hotel Stygg at the bottom of the west ridge of Styggedalstind or in the saddle between Sentraltind and Vetle Skagastølstind. The latter offers better escape possibilities and usually water in the summer. For further information refer also to Sentraltind (pages 31-32) and Store Skagastølstind (pages 22-25). Any escape from the central sections of this two day traverse could be desperate should the weather deteriorate. As such a bombproof good weather forecast is essential before embarking.

Styggedalstind seen from Sentraltind. The west top, which is nearest us, is the highest.

1.3 GJERTVASSTIND

The final summit ridge on Gjertvasstind may sometimes be covered in an ice ridge which extends onto the rock on the south side. If it does so and is icy, crampons may be essential.

Gjertvasstind, 2351m, is a huge wedge shaped ridge and marks the east end of the Styggedals ridge. Often touted as the longest uphill stretch in Norway with its 1600m ascent, it is actually short of the 1850m ascent on Skåla. It is none the less a long day with some interesting scrambling and sensational views.

THE ROUTE FROM SKOGADALSBØEN LODGE		
⇄ **18** KM	↕ **1600** M	⏱ **9-12** HRS

RATING	SEASON	SKIING	GLACIER	CLIMBING	WEATHER
7	❄ ☀ / JUL APR AUG MAY SEPT				

From Skogadalsbøen head north along the marked track **Hu.4** to Turtagrø for 2km until you get to the bridge over the river Utla. Cross the bridge to the west side and continue west along the path **Hu.4** for about 600m until the path forks with a smaller branch heading southwards. Take this branch, **Hu.15**, for about 200m until you get to the Gjertvasselvi stream. There is a ladder here down to a rock ledge where a large flat stone spans half the river. The other half is usually easy except when it is in flood, when the submerged stepping stone cannot be seen.

Once over the stream follow a faint path west up the south side of the river for 1km until it disappears. The route then starts to climb the steepish grassy slopes up to the saddle between knoll 1312m and the main ridge; it is probably best to keep to the west edge of this grassy slope. On reaching the saddle the vegetation starts to disappear and bare rock and stones become prominent. Head up the broad ridge in a westerly direction for a good 2km until you reach some large snowfields which are the remnants of the glacier to the west of knoll 1764m. Head up these sustained snow slopes for 1km until you reach the more prominent knoll 1924m.

From knoll 1924m you can look west across a small saddle to a rock band. Below this rock band to the south is another greatly diminished glacier. The route goes across the saddle and to the northern edge of the rock band. At the foot of the northern edge there are some cairns. This marks the start of the route up across the rock band which ascend diagonally in a south west direction up across some 200m when it climbs about five 5m rock steps. The cairns continue up through the rock band. There are some interesting scrambling sections here but nothing more than grade II. This scramble takes you to the top of knoll 1982m.

From the top of knoll 1982m head initially south west then veer westwards for a gentle kilometre to the base of the final summit ridge. This summit ridge rises about 250m in height over a half kilometre at an angle of about 30 degrees. In the early summer it will be covered in snow. As the summer progresses it melts, sometimes forming ice. There is often a rock ridge to the south of this snow ridge that is bare. However, during the early summer this rock ridge may disappear under the snow/ice ridge towards the top, forcing one to go on the steep snow/ice ridge. This may necessitate crampons and an ice axe is always essential. At the top of the ridge the terrain levels off onto the summit area and a stunning view which has been hiding behind Gjertvasstind suddenly unfolds over Hurrungane.

The return is by the same route unless you are continuing west along the ridge. To do this, descend to Gjertvasskardet saddle as described below in the alternative routes section then continue up to Styggedalstind as described on pages 26-27. It should be noted that to continue along the ridge is a much more serious journey than the ascent from Skogadalsbøen lodge.

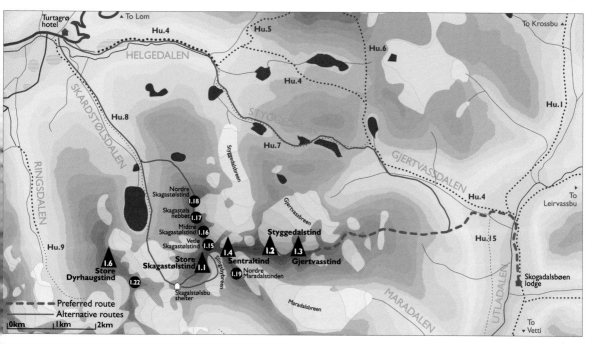

Alternative Routes

Gjertvasstind is usually climbed as a day trip from Skogadalsbøen lodge, and this is the route I have described in the preferred section. It is also rarely climbed from the saddle to the west, Gjertvasskardet, usually in conjunction with the traverse of the whole Styggedals ridge. I describe the route from this saddle to the summit for the purposes of this greater ridge traverse. See Styggedalstind (pages 26-27), Sentraltind (pages 30-31) and Skagastølstind (pages 22-25) for the other sections of this ridge.

From Gjertvasskardet ascend diagonally north west for 50-100m, passing under the steep buttress at the bottom of the west ridge of Gjertvasstind. Be wary of the bergschrund along here, which is usually quite small. This takes you to the bottom of a steep snow slope of about 45 degrees which is climbed for about 80 vertical metres. This snow slope often becomes icy during the summer as it melts and crampons are essential while snow/ice protection is often required. Slabs of exposed wet rock begin to appear interspersed amongst the ice as the summer progresses but these are treacherous. These icy patches usually persist throughout the summer. After climbing the 80m it is best to veer south towards the west ridge again as the gradient eases for the last 20m towards the summit.

If descending to Gjertvasskardet from the summit reverse the ascent route given above, or alternatively descend the snow slopes to the north of the crest of the west ridge for 30 vertical metres then head onto the crest of the ridge itself. From here head down the crest of the west ridge across often wet, exposed slab formations where up to two abseils of 30m may be required to gain easy snow slopes above the saddle. Again, snow and ice conditions may vary widely on this exposed descent. It is a good hour to ascend or descend from the saddle to the summit.

Any escape from the central sections of this two day traverse could be desperate should the weather deteriorate. As such a bombproof good weather forecast is essential before embarking.

Gjertvasstind has an interesting scrambling section before the summit ridge.

The final section ridge of the east ridge of Gertvasstind seen from Sognefjellsveien road. The steep west face can be seen on the right.

1.4 SENTRALTIND

Sentraltind in morning light seen from the saddle with Styggedalstind. The ridge on the left is Maradals ridge, the ridge coming towards us is Styggedals ridge and the ridge going away is Skagastøls ridge.

Sentraltind, 2348m, is a steep sided fortress and the meeting point of three ridges: the Styggedals ridge, the Skagastøls ridge and the Maradals ridge, all of which are sharp arêtes requiring climbing skills to traverse. Consequently Sentraltind is arguably the most difficult of all the 2000m mountains in Scandinavia.

THE ROUTE FROM TURTAGRØ HOTEL

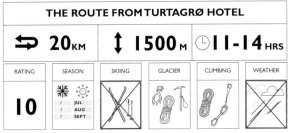

	20 KM		1500 M		11-14 HRS

RATING	SEASON	SKIING	GLACIER	CLIMBING	WEATHER
10	JUL AUG SEPT				

Leave Turtagrø hotel and follow route **Hu.8** up to Skagastølsbu shelter. This route initially crosses the road then river before continuing up to the Tindeklubhytta. Continue on the east of the river through a boulder field while climbing up above the lake to reach the edge of the glacier. The glacier is a little more than 1km and although relatively crevasse free does have a large bergschrund, which is best avoided on the west side. Glacial equipment is necessary. At the top of the glacier on the south side of the saddle is Skagastølsbu shelter, which is about three hours from Turtagrø.

From this shelter descend for a very short section down into Midtmaradalen until you reach a noticeable shelf called Berges chausée which heads east under the south face of Storen for about 1km almost horizontally to the edge of the Slingsbybreen glacier. At the edge of the glacier rope up and don crampons then start to head up the fissured glacier.

The gradient of the glacier is 25 degrees initially, however, during the lower ½km it steepens to 35 degrees and is quite fissured. At the top of this ½km section the shrinkage of the glacier has exposed a band of slabs. They are up to 40 degrees steep and often wet. They

can be difficult to pass to gain the upper section of the glacier. Early in the summer these slabs will still be covered by snowfields and will be much easier, but will certainly be exposed by mid August. The upper section of the Slingsbybreen is about 35-40 degrees and while this section is far less crevassed it can be covered in hard icy snow. At the top of this upper section is the historic Mohns skard saddle, which is about three to four hours from Skagastølsbu shelter.

To continue to Sentraltind it is not necessary to climb up the north ridge of Vetle Skagastølstind, which involves two pitches of grade IV and then V respectively, as it is possible to traverse across some ill defined shelves on the south face of this peak to reach the saddle with Sentraltind. These shelves, which are snow covered until mid summer, run in a rough horizontal line from saddle to saddle with the occasional grade II step. If going the other direction the shelves can be tricky to locate on the eastern side of the traverse, but it is best to start to traverse out just above the west side of this eastern saddle.

From this saddle between Vetle Skagastølstind and Sentraltind the west ridge of Sentraltind begins with a steep 25m grade IV pitch during which it is best to follow the ridge line itself. Once the top of this step has been gained it is an exciting but easy walk up the airy arête for 3-400m to reach the flat summit.

The return can be by the same way. Alternatively it is very feasible to descend Maradals ridge to the south east as described below and return to the Skagastølsbu shelter via this top. Two considerably longer alternatives are to return to Skagastølsbu shelter via Mohns skard again and then go over Storen, as described on page 25, or to return to Turtagrø via the Skagastøls ridge over Vetle, Midtre and Nordre Skagastølstind, as described on pages 24-25.

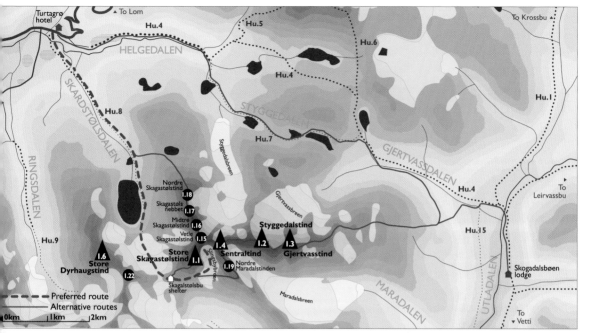

Turtagrø hotel
To Lom
HELGEDALEN
Hu.4
Hu.5
Hu.6
To Krossbu
Hu.1
Hu.4
Hu.8
STYGGEDALEN
Styggedalsbreen
Hu.7
GJERTVASSDALEN
Hu.4
To Leirvassbu
Nordre Skagastølstind **1.18**
Skagastøls nebbet **1.17**
Gjertvassbreen
Midtre Skagastølstind **1.16**
Vetle Skagastølstind **1.15**
Styggedalstind
Hu.15
RINGSDALEN
Hu.9
1.4 **1.2** **1.3**
Store Skagastølstind **1.1** **Sentraltind** **Gjertvasstind**
Skogadalsbøen lodge
1.6 **Store Dyrhaugstind**
Slingsbybreen
1.19 Nordre Maradalstinden
1.22
Skagastølsbu shelter
Maradalsbreen
MARADALEN
UTLADALEN
To Vetti
SKARDSTØLSDALEN

- - - Preferred route
— Alternative routes
0km   1km   2km

Alternative Routes

Sentraltind can be climbed via a number of routes, none of them easy. Perhaps the easiest of the three saddles to ascend from is the west one at the end of the Skagastøls ridge. However, getting to this saddle is no mean feat and the three possible routes, namely 1) the entire Skagastøls ridge from the north, 2) over Storen or 3) up the Slingsbybreen glacier, all require extensive mountaineering skills. Number 3) via Slingsbybreen glacier up to Mohns skard saddle involves the least climbing and this is the route which I describe as the preferred ascent route. This route is also a good escape route if you need to get down from the central section of the Styggedals-Skagastøls ridge if caught out by bad weather or a thunder storm. Routes 1) and 2) over the Skagastøls ridge and Storen respectively to the saddle to the west of Sentraltind are described on the Store Skagastølstind pages 24-25.

The routes from the other two saddles on the Styggedals ridge and Maradals ridge involve slightly harder climbing and these saddles are also difficult to get to. The ascent from the saddle with Styggedalstind is used when making a traverse of the whole Styggedals ridge with the usual continuation to Skagastøls ridge as well. This saddle is gained from the east by passing over both Gjertvasstind and Styggedalstind, a trip that is likely to take a day one way. For information about these two mountains please refer to the Gjertvasstind and Styggedalstind decriptions (pages 26-29). At the west end of this long saddle the steep ridge of Sentraltind begins sharply. The first (grade IV) of four pitches begins with a very exposed traverse across the north face over broken terrain for about 10m before climbing up cracks and broken corners, which may be snow and ice filled, making it harder, for another 20m to gain a flat area which is 20m long. The second pitch (grade III) starts at the end of the short flat section and goes up the north edge of the arête on some solid flakes for about 25m. The third pitch (grade II) continues up the northern edge of the arête for about 30m up a set of natural steps. The final pitch (grade III) goes up the south side of the arête, initially on a debris filled shelf for 5m and then up solid rock for the remaining 25m, to gain the flat rock plateau of the summit. Protection is essential up this ascent especially, on the first pitch.

The ascent from the saddle with Nordre Maradalstind on the Maradals ridge is also grade IV. This route is usually done in conjunction with Nordre Maradalstind from Skagastølsbu shelter or Turtagrø hotel. From Skagastølsbu shelter descend into Midtmaradalen for a very short section and then locate a wide shelf which heads east under the south face of Storen. This shelf, called Merges chausée runs for about 1km almost horizontally to the edge of the Slingsbybreen glacier, and has a couple of grade II sections. At the edge of the glacier rope up, don crampons and start to head up the fissured glacier. When on Slingsbybreen try to locate a rake descending from just to the south of the twin Nordre Maradals peaks in a north westerly direction down to the east

side of Slingsbybreen. Head over the glacier, which is significantly crevassed at this level, for the bottom of this rake. Once over the glacier follow snowfields and slabs up to the rake and ascend it to the top of the ridge on the south side of Nordre Maradalstind's southern peak. The climb up the southern peak is quite straightforward; however, the route up to the higher northern top goes over a short grade III crag, a grade III slab and then a grade IV crag, which is most easily climbed via a crack on the east side. From the top of Nordre Maradalstind descend steeply and then follow the arête north to the foot of Sentraltind. There are two choices for the final climb up to Sentraltind. Either head via the west side of the main arête where there is a steep and loose rake (grade III) which can be followed all the way to the upper part of the west arête from Skagastøls ridge and is easily followed to the top. Alternatively the Maradals ridge can be followed, where there is about 200m of scrambling and climbing up to grade IV.

Sentraltind is often climbed as part of the classic traverse from Skogadalsbøen lodge to Turtagrø over both Styggedals ridge and Skagastøls ridge which takes two long days and a night's bivouac. If it is ascended this way you climb the east ridge from the saddle with Styggedalstind as described above and descend the west ridge to the saddle with Vetle Skagastølstind, also described above. It is common to bivouac at one of these saddles if doing the entire traverse. The western saddle offers better escape options should the weather deteriorate. The best escape option is down Slingsbybreen glacier and the ascent up this is described above.

Peaks associated with Sentraltind

Nordre Maradalstind seen from Sentraltind.

1.19 Nordre Maradalstind

Nordre Maradalstind, 2160m, is climbed with some difficulty from Skagastølsbu shelter or Turtagrø hotel. It is not an easy peak by any means and involves crossing a fissured glacier and some climbing up to grade IV. It is usually climbed in conjunction with an ascent of Sentraltind via Maradals ridge and a description of that is given above in the alternative route section.

1.5 AUSTANBOTNTIND

The lofty summit ridge of Store Austanbotntind with its characteristic three humps. The peak in the middle right of the photo is Vestre Austanbotntind, and on the right is the glacier filled 45 degree gully descending down to Berdalsbreen.

Austanbotntind, 2204m, dominates the west half of Hurrungane. Its lofty exposed summit, with the three humps, rises some 700m straight above the Gravdalen valley below on the east side. From the summit ridge, the jagged south and west arêtes descend down to the south and west peaks respectively.

THE ROUTE FROM BERDALSBANDET TOLLBOOTH

⇆ 11 KM   ↕ 950 M   ⏱ 7-10 HRS

RATING	SEASON	SKIING	GLACIER	CLIMBING	WEATHER
8	JUL / AUG / SEPT				

From the parking opportunity on the old road 300m north of the toll booth on the Turtagrø to Årdal road head south up the steep slopes to pass two small tarns and gain a view of knoll 1492m and Store Austanbotntind. Head for knoll 1492m, passing slightly to the north and continue up the slabs of the rounded ridge in a north east direction to gain the main west ridge itself. This ridge can be followed all the way to a peak at 2020m quite easily with just the occasional easy scrambling section. Just to the east of this peak is a steep glacier filled gully which descends down to Berdalsbreen on the north side. The descent of this 45 degree gully has become something of a classic ski for the hardcore. The route from peak 2020m down to the top of the gully is steep and involves a short, straightforward 10m scramble. From the top of the gully the route continues east along the main ridge, with some further easy scrambling to Vestre Austanbotntind at about 2100m.

From Vestre Austanbotntind it is now easy to see the route to Austanbotntind, which looks more daunting than it is from this foreshortened aspect. There is initially a steep 40m drop down to the level saddle. A couple of sections on the descent are very steep for 5m but crampon scratches show the way. The level saddle is followed for about 200m until a thin blade of rock rises up. This

blade is very airy, and while it is possible to follow its apex, it is usual to avoid it on the south side by dropping down marginally and then following a series of vague ledges. These ledges slowly lead up towards the notch between the blade and the 45-50 degree rock/snow slab at the top of which is the summit ridge itself.

This notch on the far (east) side of the blade heralds the start of the most difficult section up a slab on the north face. There is a snow patch on the north face which varies in size. In the early summer it will completely cover the slab right to its west edge. As the summer progresses this snowfield will both melt and become icy, but slowly the western edge of the slab becomes exposed. The route goes up this slab keeping to the western edge for a 30m grade II pitch until the rock becomes broken. If the snowfield encroaches onto this western edge of the slab then an ice axe, crampons and protection are necessary. The second pitch, which is also 30m, now veers slightly to the east (left) and initially follows

Climbing the slabs. The snowfield on the left often extends onto the slabs in the early summer.

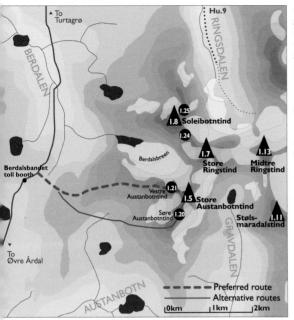

considerably as you approach a peak. Just before this peak, the route initially goes to the east of a boulder, across a narrow exposed shelf under the boulder itself. After this boulder the route then cuts back to the west side of the ridge and follows a small and equally exposed shelf past a 2m step to gain the top. This short section is grade II and due to the exposure should be protected. From the top of this the gendarme beyond and the large crag beyond that present a daunting sight.

From the top of this first peak there is a short, but narrow and exposed, arête down to the saddle with the gendarme. The gendarme itself is some 10m high and it is easiest to go over it rather than round it. The climb up is quite an easy grade III scramble, but towards the top the holds are poor and one must rely on friction, which will make things more difficult in the wet. At the top of the gendarme there is a short 7m abseil down the north side. If coming the other way this short north side is a grade V climb. From the bottom of the north side of the gendarme the direct route now goes up an easy but exposed 30m slab to the bottom of a very daunting crag and then climbs this crag for a 30m grade V pitch. The normal way up avoids this difficult crag by ascending the apex of the arête for a few metres and then traversing some 40m out to the east across the exposed slab, which drops steeply down to Gravdalen in an uninterrupted sweep. This traverse leads you under the buttress to its east ridge, beyond which is another smaller slab. This second slab, however, is often wet due to a melting snowfield. If it is wet it is probably best not to cross it but to climb the grade III pitch up the east edge of the buttress. If it *is* dry, however, it is preferable to cross this second slab and then follow the loose spur up for a grade II pitch. At the top of either of these pitches the route now follows the arête north for a problem free 100m to the top of Søre Austanbotntind.

From the top of Søre Austanbotntind the route continues north over a sensational arête, descending some 30m to the saddle with Store Austanbotntind. The descent to this saddle offers some scrambling at grade II, and although exposed is not technical. From the saddle, however, the direct route up the arête is much more demanding and involves four pitches, with three of them at grade V. This direct route is avoided by taking the normal route which is grade III. This normal route starts at the saddle and descends slightly to a small sloping shelf on the east of the arête. This broken exposed shelf continues for a short rope length across the east side of the mountain until it approaches a spur. The traverse across this broken shelf is a good grade III and route finding can be a problem as the shelves are difficult to link up. As the spur is approached the route now starts to climb up stacked blocks in a shallow gully. At the top of this gully make the short traverse to the apex of the spur. Once on the spur continue to traverse onto its south side then ascend up the loose terrain, which soon becomes more stable, for a long grade II pitch to reach the top of the lowest and most western of the three humps on the summit ridge. From this western top it is a short descent to the saddle where the normal route via the west ridge is met at the top of the large slabs on the north side. The route to the summit follows the summit ridge east described above. The total time to the summit is 7-10 hours.

a 15cm high edge between two slabs for 10m. At the top of these two slabs there is some small loose scree and this is followed for a couple of metres to the east until firmer rock is reached. This firmer rock can be followed for the remaining 15m to the lowest saddle on the summit ridge. The second pitch is grade II in the dry, but becomes grade III in the wet. This saddle is the point where the south ridge route meets the west ridge route.

From this lower saddle, the summit ridge is followed east for 50m up to the middle hump top, which is quite exposed for the last few metres and could warrant use of the rope again, especially in the wet. From the middle hump to the highest and eastern hump is another 50m which are somewhat easier. However, from the highest hump there is a little spur of about 10m to the summit. This spur consists of two narrow boulders on their edge with a large boulder at the far end on them, upon which is the summit cairn. This spur is extremely exposed and the rope should be used again here.

The return is by the same route, unless you are continuing to do the traverse of the whole mountain by descending the more challenging south ridge, in which case you add 4 hours to the time.

Alternative Routes

There are two usual routes up Store Austanbotntind: both start from the Turtagrø to Årdal road and then respectively go up the west arête via the west peak or up the south arête via the south peak. The west ridge is the normal route up and the climbing is not so demanding at grade II, but it is exposed. This west ridge is the route which I have described in the main section. The south ridge is more demanding and exposed and the climbing is up to grade IV, with long sections of grade III, and this is described here. There is a classic traverse of the whole mountain taking in the south and west ridge. This traverse is probably best done by ascending the south ridge and descending the west ridge. Ideally the traverse is best done in August when it should take 11-13 hours.

From the parking opportunity some hundred metres north of the toll booth head up to knoll 1492m as described abve. From this knoll continue east, descending into an easy corrie and crossing pleasant terrain to the rounded ridge of moraine on the east side. Climb up this moraine ridge until you get onto the ridge itself at the bottom of a steep shoulder. It is best to keep well to the south of this shoulder where the gradient is not as steep, until you gain the small plateau on top of it. From this plateau continue up the relentless boulders of the broad south ridge for another 300m until the ridge narrows

Peaks associated with Austanbotntind

Austanbotntind from near Murane on the Turtagrø to Årdal road.

1.20 Søre Austanbotntind

Søre Austanbotntind, 2103m, is a difficult peak which involves climbing up to grade IV. It can be climbed on its own, via the south ridge, but it is sometimes also climbed as part of the traverse over the whole Austanbotntind massif. This traverse is described above in the alternative routes sections.

1.21 Vestre Austanbotntind

Vestre Austanbotntind, 2100m, lies on the west ridge of Austanbotntind. It is easily climbed from the toll booth on the Turtagrø to Årdal road. It is usually climbed en route to Store Austanbotntind and is described above.

1.6 DYRHAUGSTIND

Dyrhaugstind seen from near Turtagrø. The summit is on the right and the arête leads south to the pyramid shape of Søre Dyrhaugstind and down to Skardstølsbandet on the left.

Dyrhaugstind, 2147m, is a long ridge with a few peaks along its length, which lies on the north side of Hurrungane. The summit is one of the easier mountains in the Hurrungane; however, the last half kilometre requires scrambling with some degree of exposure.

THE ROUTE FROM TURTAGRØ HOTEL

⇆ **14** KM   ↕ **1270** M   🕐 **6-8** HRS

RATING	SEASON	SKIING	GLACIER	CLIMBING	WEATHER
4	❄ ☀ FEB JUN MAR JUL APR AUG MAY SEPT				

From Turtagrø hotel take the path, **Hu.8**, for 2km towards the Skagastølsbu shelter. After a rise, and about 100m below a small dam, the path to Dyrhaugstind crosses over to the west bank of the stream. The path now goes west under steep ground to a small tarn at 1176m by Nedre Dyrhaug knoll, 1207m. After this point the path becomes barely discernable and it is best to follow a south east direction up through easy soft ground to ascend the ridge. Once on the ridge follow it up to two small tarns beyond the Øvre Dyrhaug knoll, 1435m.

Alternatively is it even easier with transport to drive the 3km up to the entrance of Ringsdalen valley and park somewhere up the small side road. From the parking place cross the small dam and then head up through the willow scrub for a few hundred metres until you reach the small saddle between the knoll of Nedre Dyrhaug and the main mountain. Don't go as far as the tarn 1176m but just head up the ridge to Øvre Dyrhaug and the two small tarns beyond. From here the path all but disappears, although stone cairns can be seen from time to time. Initially the going is tedious over large scree, but further up the ridge the stones get smaller and the going gets easier. At this stage there is a large snowfield on the east of the ridge which, if firm, might be easier to ascend. This snowfield stops short of the top and the stony apex of the narrowing ridge can be followed to the first top, Nordre Dyrhaugstind. Here at this top a magnificent view suddenly unfolds over Hurrungane and the arête to the summit can be seen for the first time.

From Nordre Dyrhaugstind, which is marked by a stone cairn, the ridge narrows considerably for the last 300m to the main summit. There is a fair degree of exposure on this section, and in the spring when covered in snow a rope and some slings will add confidence for those who are not used to it. Heading south the ridge initially drops slightly and narrows for 100m until there is a very narrow section which leads to a 3m step. This step is best passed on the west side, where a rock spike offers a good hold and leads to an easy 10m, 45 degree shelf with further good holds, up to a small peak sometimes called Rygtind. From Rygtind, the ridge drops marginally and then levels out for 100m before rising up a 5m slab to another narrow section. This section is best passed by scrambling up the slab and crossing over to the west before ascending a 15m, 45 degree shelf with good holds which leads to the summit and its huge cairn.

The continuation south along the ridge for 1km over the other tops to Søre Dyrhaugstind offers more of the same exciting but quite manageable scrambling for those with some experience, if the weather is dry. It takes about an hour to traverse the ridge from Store to Søre Dyrhaugstind. Unless you are both experienced and equipped you will have to return via the ridge to Nordre Dyrhaugstind and then down the north ridge again. On the descent it is best to make use of the large snowfield on the east side of this north ridge. Do not go to far to the east as there is a huge drop down to Skardstølsdalen. At the bottom of this snowfield bear west to avoid the large cliff and head to the two small tarns at Øvre Dyrhaug knoll. From here follow the same route used for the ascent.

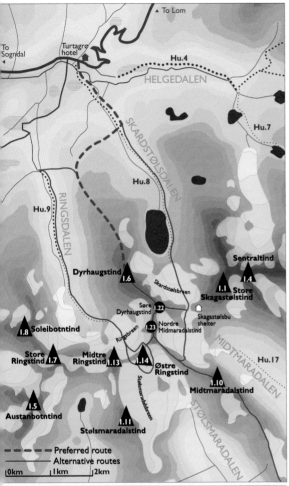

Alternative Routes

Dyrhaugstind is usually climbed from Turtagrø (or from the entrance to Ringsdalen) and this route is described under the preferred ascent section. There are also two classic traverses along the ridge. The first (1) is from Turtagrø to Skagastølsbu shelter, then steeply up to Søre Dyrhaugstind and north along the ridge to Dyrhaugstind before descending the broad north ridge to Turtagrø. The second (2) is from Turtagrø along the ridge from Nordre to Søre Dyrhaugstind and then across Berges skard saddle to the peak of Nordre Midtmaradalstind. From here descend west to the saddle with Østre Ringstind and then abseil down the north side of the saddle to Ringsbreen glacier and thereafter Ringsdalen. It is also possible to abseil down the south side of this saddle onto Stolsmaradalsbreen glacier and then round Østre Ringstind to reach Ringsskard. There is a third (3) very demanding traverse over both Dyrhaugstind and then Midtmaradalstind.

1. The traverse over Dyrhaugs ridge, from Søre to North Dyrhaugstind, involves some grade V climbing and is really beyond the scope of this book, but as it is such a classic I have included it. The traverse starts from Skagastølsbu shelter. To get there follow **Hu. 8** for the three hours. From here head west up the arête for an hour, with some easy scrambling, to the bottom of the imposing 200m crag. This crag is six pitches. The lower two are 30m each and go up some 5m to the south of the apex of the arête, and are grade III. Then the route traverses across a shelf to the south for a rope length to a large flake. The next pitch, which is the hardest at grade V, weaves up for 30m passing between two blocks to a stance. From here there are another two pitches, each of 40m at grade IV, to reach the top of Søre Dyrhaugstind. From this peak head north initially with an easy 300m walk down the boulders on the north flank of Søre Dyrhaugstind to the saddle with Midtre Dyrhaugstind. From this saddle the 300m walk up to the southern of the two Midtre Dyrhaugstind tops is initially quite straight forward, but it soon narrows into an exciting arête with some scrambling for the last section. The ridge north from here to the northern

Midtre Dyrhaugstind, and indeed on to Store Dyrhaugstind itself, continues to be exposed and airy with many scrambling sections at grade II. The obstacles encountered can be avoided on the west side on scree overlooking Ringsdalen. From Store Dyrhaugstind to Nordre Dyrhaugstind the scrambling continues for 300m before the long easy descent down the north flank of the mountains as described in the preferred section. This circuit from Turtagrø takes 9-11 hours.

2. The traverse from Turtagrø to Nordre Midtmaradalstind goes up Dyrhaugstind as described in the preferred section and then continues to Søre Dyrhaugstind as described in reverse above. From here head down the south ridge which after an initial easy section turns into steep slabs. At the bottom of these slabs there is a loose section before the ridge becomes more of an arête with a fair bit of scrambling until Berges skard saddle is reached. At the saddle there is a 3m notch which is best tackled on the west side. After the tricky scramble out of the notch the north arête of Nordre Midtmaradalstind is a reasonably straightforward grade II scramble to a subsidary top. Beyond this top to the south is the main peak across a small saddle without difficulties. While this traverse is usually done without protection in the dry, it should warrant the use of a rope in the wet or with snow. The easiest return is by the same route; however, it is possible to descend the south west ridge of Nordre Midtmaradalstind to the saddle with Østre Ringstind. From this saddle there is a 50m abseil down the north side on 45 degree slabs recently exposed by the diminishing Ringsbreen glacier and onto this glacier, where there may be a bergschrund. Once on the crevassed glacier descend west down the wind formed snow ridge under the north face of Østre Ringstind towards Ringsskard saddle, until you intercept the route **Hu.18** from Stølsmaradalen cabin to Turtagrø. Follow this route down into Ringsdalen as described. This round trip from Turtagrø is about 10-12 hours.

3. It is possible to descend the south ridge of Nordre Midtmaradalstind to Lovskard saddle. This is a more demanding route and is only suitable for very experienced parties. The south ridge involves climbing to grade III, not including the difficult pinnacles which are avoided on the west side. The pinnacles can all be most easily climbed from the north side, but the most northerly one is grade V. At the bottom of the south ridge is Lovskard saddle which can be descended on the east side via a 40 degree snow/ice filled gully down to Midtmaradalsbreen glacier. The crevassed glacier is then crossed in a north direction to reach the Skagastølsbu shelter and bandet, before then heading down to Turtagrø. Allow an 11-13 hours round trip from Turtagrø. For those wanting a very demanding, but superb high level traverse, right across Hurrungane, it is possible to continue from Lovskard saddle up Midtmaradalstind and then down to Stølsmaradalen cabin. Details of this route from Lovskard south over Midtmaradalstind are given on the Midtmaradalstind pages (42-43). This traverse takes around 20 hours.

Peaks associated with Dyrhaugstind

Dyrhaugstind from Midtmaradalstind to the south.

1.22 Søre Dyrhaugstind

Søre Dyrhaugstind, 2072m, lies on the Dyrhaugs ridge to the south of the highest part of the ridge. It can be ascended most easily via a traverse along this ridge from Store Dyrhaugstind as described above. It can also be climbed from the Bandet via the eastern arête and a difficult but classic grade V 200m six pitch climb up the steep buttress on this arête.

1.23 Nordre Midtmaradalstind

Nordre Midtmaradalstind, 2062m, is at the very south end of Dyrhaugs ridge beyond Berges skard saddle. It is

most easily ascended via this ridge and saddle as described above. For very experienced parties it is also possible to climb it from Lovskard saddle via the south ridge. This saddle is approached from Turtagrø and the Bandet by crossing the Midtmaradalsbreen and then climbing a 35 degree snow/ice filled gully. From the saddle, the south ridge involves grade III climbing. The four pinnacles that are encountered are grade V, but they can be avoided on the west side. The return to Turtagrø can be via the entire Dyrhaugs ridge as described above. Allow 12 hours for the trip from Turtagrø via Lovskard and back to Turtagrø via the ridge.

1.7 STORE RINGSTIND

Store Ringstind from the top of the rock band in Ringsdalen. The picture shows the icefall and the glacial ramp up the east flank above this icefall. In such conditions, in the middle spring, the danger of crevasses is diminished and the mountain is a fantastic ski trip.

Store Ringstind, 2124m, is one of the most characteristic mountains in Norway. Almost vertical on three sides, the fourth side is a 35-40 degree slope covered in a glacier, and it looks like a huge wedge. Store Ringstind is an exceptionally good mountain for a spring ski ascent, particularly in early May.

THE ROUTE FROM TURTAGRØ HOTEL

⇆ 16 KM	↕ 1200 M	◔ 8-10 HRS

RATING	SEASON	SKIING	GLACIER	CLIMBING	WEATHER
7	MAR JUL APR AUG MAY SEPT				

From Turtagrø drive the 3km on the small road to Årdal until there is a rough gravel road heading south up Ringsdalen for ½km. Park somewhere here, head down to the river and cross the dam and pick up the path on the east side. This path follows the river for 3km across pleasant level meadows with the spectacular view of Store and Midtre Ringstind at the end. After 3km the path reaches a braided gravel bed in the river and shortly afterwards leaves the meadow and enters a boulder field. Continue through this boulder field for a further kilometre until you reach a small lake. After this lake you are surrounded by moraine but the boulder field on the west (right) is actually sitting on top of the melting snout of the glacier. Follow the edge of the glacier for another km through more boulders until the going gets easier and the rocks smaller. From here, in the summer, two snowfields should be visible below cliffs on the east side of the valley, one with waterfalls beside it and the other further north without waterfalls. It is the latter one to now aim for up a scree covered slope. This snowfield varies in size according to how the previous winter's snowfall has been and the time in summer. If the snowfield has melted to the extent that rock band is exposed at the top, then it is perhaps easiest to ascend the snowfield directly and then climb out of the steeper rock band at

the top on the southern side. The climb up the rock band is steep and wet and is grade II. From the top of this snowfield or rock band the route descends slightly south east for ½km across flat moraine until you reach the edge of the glacier. On the return journey do not head down too soon to find the route down the rock band as it is surprisingly far to the north. This route is marked by cairns.

Due to the glacial environs of Store and Midtre Ringstind it is not possible to do these mountains solo during the late spring and summer time. Indeed, parties should not only have glacial experience and equipment, but also some rescue knowledge and pulleys to carry out any crevasse rescue. At the edge of the glacier

Looking south up Ringsdalen to Store Ringstind.

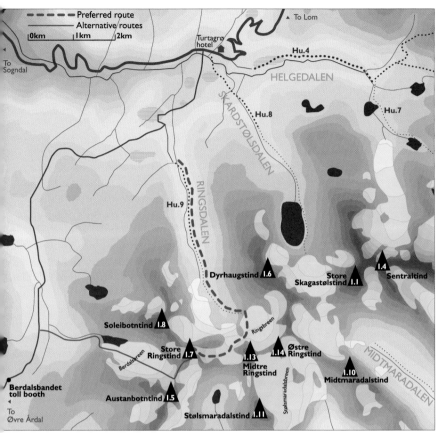

The view from the summit is magnificent. Store Skagastølstind to the north east has a wonderful symmetry with the Skagastøls ridge on the left and the Styggedals ridge on the right. Particularly impressive also is Austanbotntind to the south west with its fearsome cliffs. The return is by the same route. It should be easily possible to combine an ascent of Store Ringstind with an ascent of Midtre Ringstind in the summer from the heavily crevassed Gravdalskard saddle between them. If ascending Midtre Ringstind also, allow an extra two and a half hours. For more details see the Midtre Ringstind pages (48-49).

Perhaps the best time to ascend Store Ringstind is in middle spring during the last half of April and the first half of May. The problems of the summer, i.e. the steep wet rock band, the extensive crevasses and the steep blue ice and loose scree just before the summit are significantly diminished. The last 300m are too steep to ascend on skis and these are normally left while the final section is done on foot. The descent is truly magnificent, but some sections are quite steep for most mortals.

you should prepare for this glacier travel. Initially the route is towards Ringsskard saddle to the south but veers to the south west so as to pass the lower edge of the glacier directly north of Midtre Ringstind. While crossing this part of the glacier you should pay extra special attention to stones rolling down from the steeper glacier from above, especially on a warm or wet day, and it is unwise whatever the weather to pause here. Once this section of the glacier is passed continue in a south west direction, passing above an icefall to reach the flatter saddle between Store and Midtre Ringstind. This saddle is called Gravdalskard and contains many crevasses.

From Gravdalskard the route follows the glacier that comes down from Store Ringstind. In general it is slightly easier to find a route up the middle to south of the glacier but this depends on the time of year. About half way up there is often a particularly large crevasse that might stretch across the whole glacier during the late summer. Normally, the last snow bridge disappears on the very southern side. It is usually obvious to see this from further down. If this bridge has gone then it will be necessary to climb onto the rock ridge, also on the south of the glacier, and bypass the crevasse. This may not always be an easy transition due to a varying bergschrund. After this large crevasse the gradient eases and the route continues up the glacier, heading for a midpoint on the summit ridge. As the summit ridge approaches the gradient steepens again and the snowfield on the glacier's surface will invariably give way to blue ice, which may be as much as 45 degrees. A couple of ice screws could be useful here. Beyond the blue ice at the top of the glacier is the summit ridge. Late in the summer season the top of the glacier may have melted sufficiently to expose a large amount of very loose stones between the top of the blue ice and the summit ridge. Care should be taken here not to shower your partners with rocks. Once on the ridge it is an easy but quite airy short trip south along the summit ridge to the top.

Alternative Routes

Due to the shape of the mountain the only common ascent route is the east flank, and this is described above. There is a seldom used five pitch climbing route, of up to grade VI, on the south side from the Ramnaskard saddle, between Store Ringstind and Austanbotntind. This saddle is most easily gained by ascending the crevassed Berdalsbreen glacier from the Turtagrø to Årdal road. From the Ramnaskard saddle this route initially follows the south ridge until the ridge gets steep. It then traverses out onto the steep south east flank across shelves for two rope lengths. After this traverse there are two pitches up a steep gully to gain the summit ridge. Once on the summit ridge scramble north for a steep 100m to the summit.

Store Ringstind from Stølsmaradalstind. The ridge on the left is the south ridge which rises up from Ramnaskard saddle.

1.8 SOLEIBOTNTIND

Store Soleibotntind (on the right) from Berdalsfjellet. In the middle is Nordre Soleibotntind and on the left is Lauvnostind.

Soleibotntind, 2083m, is the most westerly of all the Hurrungane mountains. It retains an alpine character, and two of the three ridges are sharp jagged arêtes, but the third ridge is surprisingly gentle. The view from the summit of Soleibotntind is generally considered to be one of the best in Hurrungane.

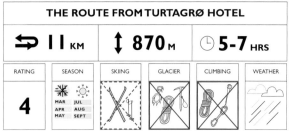

THE ROUTE FROM TURTAGRØ HOTEL

⮌ 11 KM	↕ 870 M	🕐 5-7 HRS

RATING	SEASON	SKIING	GLACIER	CLIMBING	WEATHER
4	❄ ☀ MAR JUL APR AUG MAY SEPT				

From Turtagrø hotel take the Turtagrø to Årdal road for 9km over Berdalsfjellet and then down for 1km further to the small bridge where the road goes over the Tverrelvi stream, and where it is possible to park. Follow the south side of the stream up east for ½km, then leave the stream and veer south for ½km, keeping to the east of a ridge which is starting to form. After this second ½km you should come across a small shallow tarn at about 1335m elevation. Follow the stream, which is still the Tverrelvi, east and then south for another ½km until you get to the west end of a larger tarn erroneously marked on the map as 512m, but actually about 1425m elevation.

From the west end of this lake head south up a stony spur which climbs and veers south east up onto a shoulder, called Bukkanosi, on the main west ridge. Continue up, passing slightly to the north of knoll 1674m (where there is a large cairn) until you get to the bottom of the steeper section. If making a spring ski ascent this is probably the place to leave skis as the steeper ridge is often poorly covered in snow.

The steeper section of the ridge is not marked but the route goes straight up the stony ridge for a sustained climb of nearly an hour. During this ascent try and keep to the centre of the ridge and veer to the south side as you approach a steeper rocky outcrop towards the top. Weave through this steep small outcrop to gain a much

easier gradient beyond it and then after another 200m a cairn on a false summit.

After the false summit head due east for an easy ½km of stony ground across the flattish summit dome to reach the main summit. In the spring and early summer there are large cornices on the north side of this summit area, so keep a distance from the edge.

The return is by the same route unless you are experienced and prepared (rope, crampons and an ice axe) to go down the north or south east ridges.

Although Store Soleibotntind can easily be climbed in the spring via this route, the road from Turtagrø to Årdal does usually not open until mid May. Furthermore, the west ridge is too exposed to hold much snow, so while the lower half of the described route can be done on skis, and is an excellent trip, the upper steep section is too stony and has to be done on foot.

A sunbasked Soleibotntind rises above Lauvnostind. On the left is Søre Soleibotntind, then Nordre, then the rounded Store Soleibotntind behind, with Lauvnostind on the right.

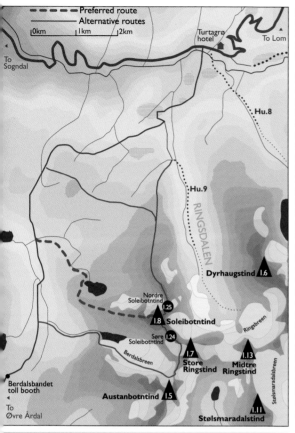

steps on the north west side. It takes about five hours from Berdalsfjellet to the summit. Add one and a half hours if Nordre Soleibotntind is included. Descend via the easy west ridge (three hours extra) or complete the classic traverse by continuing down the south east ridge as described below (five hours extra).

For the south east ridge it is best to start from the Turtagrø to Årdal road about 2km south of the bridge over the Berdalselvi river. From the road make for the glacial lake at the bottom of the Berdalsbreen glacier. Go onto the glacier well to the south of this lake and start to climb up towards Ramnaskard saddle to the east. This glacier is crevassed and glacial experience and equipment are essential. As you approach the pass the gradient steepens. From the Ramnaskard saddle head north across rocks to the detached higher section of Berdalsbreen. Continue north across this small glacier, traversing up towards Soleiskard saddle between Soleibotntind and the sheer wall of Store Ringstind on the east of the saddle. From the saddle head north west up the arête for about 50m then leave the arête on the west side and continue up across loose scree for another 100m until you are to the east of a snow field. Clamber up the loose rock on the eastern edge of this snow field. As you approach the top of the snowfield, traverse across it to the western side and then continue up across the rock to a knoll on the south end of the south east ridge itself. From here the 200m arête to Søre Soleibotntind is airy but quite straightforward. From this peak the arête north west is quite straightforward scrambling for 150m where there is a crag. This is avoided on the west side as there are vast drops on the east side. From this crag the straightforward scrambling resumes for another 300m past a small saddle and up to a small top. From this small top go back south east slightly and scramble down quite steeply on the west side (grade II) to gain a shelf. Follow this shelf north west under the small top for 30m until you reach a prominent long snow gully descending all the way to the glacier. Climb up this gully for 20 metres to reach the saddle, being aware of any cornice. From this saddle clamber up the steep slope of loose stones, with your back to the small peak, to gain the rounded summit dome. Once you are on the summit dome veer north for 300m across stones to the summit itself. It takes about 5 hours from the road to the summit. Descend via the easy west ridge (3 hours extra) or complete the classic traverse by continuing down the north ridge as described above (4 hours extra, or 5½ hours including Nordre Soleibotntind).

Alternative Routes

The west ridge is the only simple way up Soleibotntind and it is described in the main section. There are two more difficult routes also, one up the north ridge which involves some difficult scrambling/easy climbing and the route up the south east ridge which involves a glacier crossing and some difficult scrambling. These two more difficult routes are only really feasible in mid to late summer (July-mid September). The route up the north ridge was also the route of the first ascent in 1888. The two routes, up the north and south east ridges, can be combined to give a classic traverse which is likely to take experienced parties ten hours in good conditions. The traverse can always be cut short at the half way point by descending the easy west ridge.

For the north ridge it is probably best to start at Berdalsfjellet some 7km from Turtagrø hotel on the Turtagrø to Årdal road. It is also possible to start from the same road at the turn off up Ringsdalen which is just 3km from Turtagrø hotel. Whichever starting point the first objective is the knoll of Lauvnosi, 1482m, on the north ridge of Lauvnostind and Soleibotntind. Lauvnosi is 2½km to the east or south of the two starting points respectively. From Lauvnosi follow the ridge up, heading over to the east side where there is a great view down into Ringsdalen and the mountains beyond. After an easy 2 km the ridge starts to narrow considerably, with airy drops on each side for the final ½km to Lauvnostind, 1965m. After Lauvnostind the narrow ridge drops to the saddle with Nordre Soleibotntind. About 30m before the saddle there is a gully to the west with an awkward chock stone in it. Descend this grade III gully, clambering over the chock stone, and continue down the steep, short, loose gully to a shelf. Follow this shelf north round a difficult corner to reach the saddle. From this saddle Nordre Soleibotntind can be climbed up the north arête but this involves a pitch of grade V. It is possible to avoid this by skirting round to the west side of the peak. At the bottom of the crag a sloping shelf leads off south. Follow this for 100m until you are at the bottom of a wide, and probably snow filled, gully. This short gully, which is 35 degrees, may be icy and crampons are essential, if not a rope also. The top of this snow gully is at the saddle between Nordre Soleibotntind and Soleibotntind itself. Nordre Soleibotntind can be ascended from here by its south west arête (see associated peaks below for details). From the saddle scramble along and up the craggy exposed arête for 300m to Soleibotntind, avoiding a couple of

Peaks associated with Soleibotntind

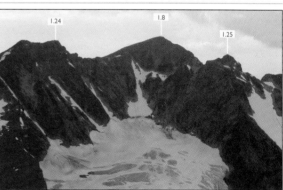

Soleibotntind from Ringskard to the east.

1.24 Søre Soleibotntind

Søre Soleibotntind, 2049m, is most easily climbed from Store Soleibotntind. From the summit of the latter head south for 300m until you are opposite a small top the other side of a deep saddle. Scrabble down the steep loose slope to this saddle (beware of cornices). At the saddle descend 20m down a snow gully, which is likely to be icy, to gain a shelf formation on the west side of the small top. Follow this shelf for 30m then start to scramble up to the ridge, gaining it south of the small top. Once on the ridge follow it south east for 400m, avoiding any obstacles by scrambling round to the west of them, until you reach the peak.

1.25 Nordre Soleibotntind

Nordre Soleibotntind, 2030m, is best climbed from the saddle between Soleibotntind and Nordre Soleibotntind. Head north east along the south west arête to the bottom of the first crag. From here the first 20m of the route goes on the exposed east side of the arête. Then there is an exposed 2m but grade V climb onto the arête, then then onto the west side. Scramble along formations (grade II) on the west side, passing under the peak, and then make the short climb (grade III) up onto the north arête. Double back and head south again now up to the airy peak. This peak necessitates rope, protection, crampons and an ice axe.

1.9 FANNARÅKEN

Fannaråken is a graceful mountain offering a variety of ascent routes.

Fannaråken, 2068m, is a graceful sweep of a mountain which has inspired poets travelling on the ancient Sognefjellsveien road. Its gently rising summit ridge emerges steeply from the Fannaråkbreen glacier on the north side. On top of the mountain is a stunningly located cabin with an outstanding view.

THE ROUTE FROM TURTAGRØ HOTEL		
⇌ **15** KM	↕ **1170** M	🕐 **7-8** HRS

RATING	SEASON	SKIING	GLACIER	CLIMBING	WEATHER
3	❄ ☀ MAR JUL APR AUG MAY SEPT				

From Turtagrø follow the main road up for 400m until the first corner past the boom. Here on the lower side of the road a rough track gently descends westwards under the main road heading into Helgedalen valley. Leave this road and take this track for a good kilometre, passing to the south of some cabins. Just after the cabins you will meet a gravel tractor track. It is possible to drive to the locked boom by these cabins, but parking is very limited and it is unfair to clog up the area so the owners of the cabins can't park.

After reaching the gravel track head up the valley for an easy, flat 2km until you come to a series of hairpin bends going up the steep rise at the end of the valley. At the fifth bend, and the last bend before the track crosses the tumbling Skauta stream, there is a sign posted path to Fannaråken and Skogadalsbøen. Take this path, which crosses a stream after 200m and then after another 200m comes to the Ekrehytta cabin. At this cabin the path forks again with a marked branch heading west below the cabin heading for Skogadalsbøen lodge, while the path up Fannaråken goes up to the west of the Ekrehytta cabin.

From the cabin the route initially climbs up beside the tumbling stream, emerging from the side valley of Steindalen for quarter of an hour. It then veers away from the stream and starts to head up the steep base of the ridge. Although steep, the path is well established and zigzags up the worst bits so there should be no problems, even in the wet. After another half hour of sustained ascent up

this steepest section the gradient eases out momentarily. From this flatter area the next section up the ridge unfolds.

This section also involves 400m of ascent but is not so steep as the previous section from Ekrehytta. The good path is on stable scree and is less arduous than it looks, and after three quarters of an hour the steep crags by Marangsgjelet start to appear on the south side. The path continues to climb skirting round the top of these crags for another quarter of an hour, until the gradient eases at the top of a false summit. From this false summit the well marked path gently climbs north west across the packed stones of the summit plateau for a final quarter of an hour to reach the cabins and just beyond the summit.

The westerly hut is the original DNT hut and the hut right on the summit is an old weather station which DNT has taken over. Just to the east of the weather station hut is a flatter area above the cliffs and glacier where there is a marvellous view over the Fannaråkbreen glacier to the Smørstabb massif and the rest of Jotunheimen beyond. Fannaråken also gives an unsurpassed view to the huge north face of the connected Styggedals and Skagastøls ridges to the south.

This route is feasible in the spring but is steep to ascend and not really enjoyable to descend due to poor snow cover and steepness. If making a spring ascent on skis the route from Sognefjellshytta across the glacier is such a classic it is the only option.

The descent can either be by the same route or via any of the other three routes. If you want to be guided down the glacier to Sognefjellshytta during July and August you must be at the cabin before 1100hrs, which means either a very early start from Turtagrø or overnighting at the very comfortable and stunningly located cabin. It is also common to spend the night at the summit cabin and then descend to Skogadalsbøen lodge the next day, although this could also easily be done in a 8-9 hour day. A return via Steindalsnosi is only suitable for the more experienced.

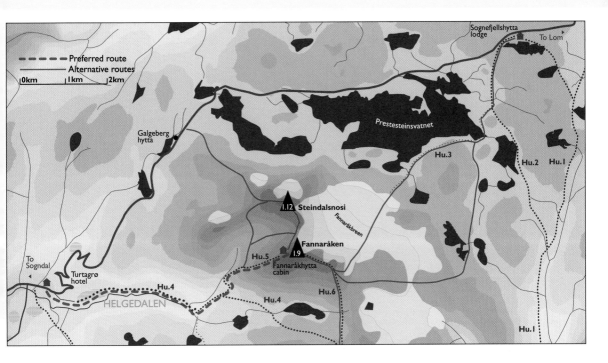

Alternative Routes

There are a number of ways up Fannaråken. The simplest way is from Turtagrø as it does not involve any glacier crossing and this is described below. The shortest way is from Sognefjellshytta lodge, but this involves a glacier crossing and the relevant experience and equipment. This short way is a fantastic route in the spring for a ski ascent. The third way is from Skogadalsbøen lodge, and while this is ideally a summer route, it is also possible in the spring on skis. Both the routes from Sognefjellshytta and from Skogadalsbøen lodges are described here. It is quite common to combine any two of these three routes to traverse the mountain in a day. There is also an unmarked route traversing over from the mountain of Steindalsnosi to the north, via a scree and boulder covered saddle, which is also described here.

From Sognefjellshytta lodge follow the route **Hu.3** round the east and then south shore of Prestesteinvatnet lake for 4km. Then leave the shore and head south for 1km to the edge of the glacier. Rope up here and then head south up the initially steep glacier. As the glacier levels off, a snow/ice ridge comes into view curving up to crags below Fannaråknosi, 1990m, at the east end of the summit ridge. Head for the base of this snow/ice ridge and then ascend the glacier to the east of it to avoid the steep slopes up to Fannaråknosi. Keep ascending the glacier to approach the south ridge of Fannaråknosi itself. The further south you go as you approach the ridge the less the final gradient onto the ridge itself is. Once on the ridge you meet the marked path from Skogadalsbøen lodge to Fannaråken, **Hu.6**, which is then followed for 2km to the summit as described in the next paragraph. This route is a classic in the spring on skis when many of the problems posed by crevasses are avoided; after late May, however, you will have to be wary of crevasses. The large cornices along the north side of the summit ridge are in constant danger of falling throughout spring and this area of the glacier below them should be avoided as it is avalanche prone at this time. There is guiding from the cabin down the glacier leaving at 1100hrs and from the bottom edge of the glacier back up at 1300hrs during the time Fannaråkhytta cabin is open in the summer (July and August). It is possible to go from Sognefjellshytta to Fannaråken without going onto the glacier. To do this follow the route to the east of Prestesteinvatnet lake for 2km then continue south for another 3km past numerous small tarns, over a small saddle and into Steindalen. Do not descend into Steindalen but head south west and then follow the shore of Øvre Steindalsvatnet lake. From the south shore of this lake head south west for 1km to the knoll 1605m. At the knoll veer west across the snow fields, which are the remnants of the glacier marked on the map but since melted, and then continue west for another 1½km to reach the south ridge which is easily gained to meet route **Hu.6**, which is followed for 2km to the summit as again described in the next paragraph. Both of these alternatives from

Sognefjellshytta take about five hours. The return can be by any of the other two ascent routes or via the saddle to the north with Steindalsnosi.

The route from Skogadalsbøen to Fannaråken is marked in the summer with cairns, and is also under the 'walking routes' section as **Hu.6**. From Skogadalsbøen head up to the Kaiser pass on the marked path which goes up Utladalen for 2km and then crosses over the permanent bridge. Once over the bridge follow the pleasant Gjertvassdalen valley up for 4km until you get to the private Gjertvassbu cabin and Gjertvatnet lake. Do not take the smaller path to the west, **Hu.7**, but continue north on the marked path for 1km up the west side of the lake and then up to the Keisarpasset saddle. Here at the saddle the path forks again. Do not take the path heading down the valley to the west and Turtagrø but continue north, skirting about 300m to the east above a small tarn. Once you have passed the tarn the marked path starts to traverse steeply up stony ground towards what looks like a saddle at the bottom of the south ridge of Fannaråknosi. Just before this perceived saddle there are some small snowfields and a small stream to cross. After crossing the stream a flat wasteland of stone and snowfield unfolds to the west rather than a drop. From here it is a sustained climb up the south ridge for about an hour to reach the top of the ridge, but as a consolation a magnificent view starts to unfold over the Smørstabb massif to the north east. As you approach the top of the ridge the glacier route from Sognefjellshytta joins from the east. The route does not actually go up to Fannaråknosi but skirts round the south side of it and reaches the summit ridge just to the west of it, where another magnificent view unfolds over the glacier far below. From this little saddle it is 1km walk westwards across what feels like the top of the world to the summit and the Fannaråkhytta cabin. During this final kilometre be wary of the cornices overhanging the huge drops to the north, and be exceptionally cautious in poor weather. This ascent takes about four to five hours. The return can be by any of the other two ascent routes or via the saddle to the north with Steindalsnosi.

A final but more demanding ascent route can combine the ascent of Steindalsnosi with Fannaråken. There are two alternatives, both unmarked and seldom used, and they are only advised for the more experienced. The direct alternative is down the steep south ridge of Steindalsnosi and then up the north ridge of Fannaråken, which gets very steep at the top for a short scrambling section. During the spring there is a cornice at the top of this scrambling section on Fannaråken and the route is not recommended. An easier alternative to this direct route is via the saddle between the summit and west top (1936m) of Steindalsnosi. From this saddle drop down the steep unpleasant stony slopes into Steindalen, cross the valley floor and then traverse south up the flank of the south west ridge of Fannaråken for a good half hour until you intersect the marked path from Turtagrø to Fannaråken, **Hu.5**. Follow this path for an hour to the summit and cabins.

1.10 MIDTMARADALSTIND

Midtmaradalstind from Østre Ringstind to the north east. The saddle on the left is Lovskard.

Midtmaradalstind, 2056m, is a seldom climbed but magnificent craggy peak in the remoter southern half of Hurrungane. The east face, at nearly 1km high, offers the 30 pitch Jubileumsveggen route. It is flanked on each side by Stølsmaradalen and Midtmaradalen, two of the very finest U shaped glacial valleys.

THE ROUTE FROM STØLSMARADALEN CABIN

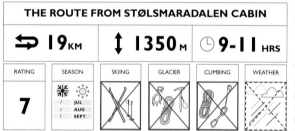

RATING	SEASON	SKIING	GLACIER	CLIMBING	WEATHER
7	❄ ☀ JUL AUG SEPT				

From Stølsmaradalen cabin follow route **Hu.16** to Skogadalsbøen lodge for half an hour or 1km, until you are half way to Snørestødet, 1220m. At this point head north up the steep hillside and veer north west as you climb up 150m. Eventually the slope eases and you can head for the outflow of Storebekkvatnet at the lake's south end. Do not be tempted to head up the hill too quickly from Stølsmaradalen cabin as the steep, densely vegetated hill is difficult to negotiate.

From Storebekkvatnet lake head north west for 1km to ascend the 300m to Stølsnosi, 1542m, where you get an exceptional panorama view over the Hurrungane massif. From Stølsnosi continue north west for a further 3km over easy undulating ground to knoll 1749m at the far end of the glacier. During the pleasant walk the view gets better still; Storen dominates the north and to the west Austanbotntind rises sharply above everything. The duo of Mannen and Kjerringi look particularly impressive from here.

From knoll 1749m the terrain becomes more challenging, starting with a steep scramble up Søre Midtmaradalstind 1958m, which is straightforward enough and gives a taste of things to come. It is an easy short descent to the west from here down to the top of a glacier which is safe and simple to cross for 300m to the saddle between the Søre and Vesle Midtmaradalstind, 2017m. Here you get

a good view of the massive, almost vertical 750m walls on the north east side of the Midtmaradals ridge down to the tranquil U shaped valley of Midtmaradalen. These walls are the biggest in Jotunheimen.

From this saddle there is a steep climb up to Vesle Midtmaradalstind. The route skirts the west side of a steep crag right at the bottom of the ridge. Once this crag has been passed the route veers east again to the apex of the main ridge and goes up steeply between this apex and a small gully parallel to it and 20m to the west. There are three bits which are quite steep but are easy. The gradient of the ridge eases considerably as it reaches Vesle Midtmaradalstind.

From the top of Vesle Midtmaradalstind the descent north west down the ridge is exposed and a grade II section needs to be downclimbed and then a steep grade II section climbed on the other side of the saddle. This exposed scramble can be avoided by descending to the west of Vesle Midtmaradalstind for 20m to gain an easier route on a shelf heading north some 10 m below the saddle on the south west side of this saddle.

From here, below the saddle, there is an obvious ledge running along the south west face of the summit peak. Follow this ledge for 40m until you reach a steep gully running up to the main ridge. The ledge continues, but leave it here and climb the gully for 25m to reach the main ridge. The lower section of this gully is very steep for 5m. Once on the main ridge follow it for five minutes to the top, negotiating one final scramble just before the main summit. The view is stunning. There is a small metal box on the summit containing a note book from the first winter ascent in 1958.

The return is by the same route. The main ridge is followed down and 30m before the saddle is a stone cairn that marks the top of the steep gully on the south west to reach the ledge 25m below, thereby avoiding the difficult and exposed saddle. Once back on the

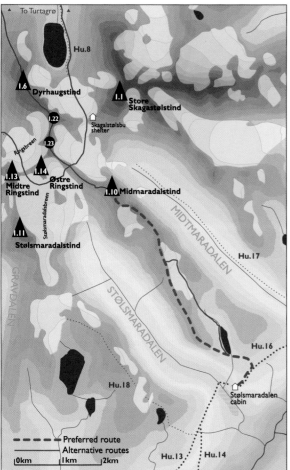

Preferred route
Alternative routes

top 1749m it is possible to follow the western edge of the glacier for ½km. Once this ½km is completed it is possible to cross the glacier safely in an easterly direction for 300m to the eastern edge. The eastern side of the glacier is now followed until you reach the glacial stream's outflow emerging from under the glacier. Care must be taken to avoid the snow bridge caused by the stream's outflow and the steeper section of glacier to the south and west of it must also be avoided as there are small crevasses here. This glacial stream can now be followed down to Storebekkvatnet lake which is best crossed on the west side. It is again best to aim just south of Snørestødet to join the Skogadalsbøen lodge to Stølsmaradalen cabin path, **Hu.16**. This will ensure avoiding the steep vegetated slopes on the south side of the ridge.

Alternative Routes

There are essentially only two options to climb Midtmaradalstind; via the simplest south east ridge or via the much more demanding north west ridge. The south east ridge can be climbed from Hjelle road end by Årdal in an extremely long and arduous day. It is more usual to break this day up by staying in the extremely charming Stølsmaradalen cabin, probably the most idyllic and picturesque of all the DNT cabins. To get to this cabin follow route **Hu.14** from Hjelle to Vetti Farm and up Brendeteigen for 4½ hours in total, or follow the routes **Hu.11** and **Hu.13** for 5 hours in total.

The ascent via the north west ridge is for very experienced parties only as it involves glacier travel, climbing to grade III and a very remote location. The climb starts at Lovskard, but even getting to Lovskard is a challenge in itself. There are three options to get to Lovskard, firstly from the east via Midtmaradalsbreen, secondly from the west via Stølsmaradalsbreen

and thirdly, the most difficult way, via the south east ridge of Nordre Midtmaradalstind and Dyrhaugstind.

The first way from the east over Midtmaradalsbreen is probably the easiest. The route starts from Turtagrø and goes up to the Skagastølsbu shelter as per **Hu.8**. From here the route initially goes south west traversing slightly down across snowfields and rock for ½km until it reaches the edge of the Midtmaradalsbreen glacier. It then veers south and traverses up across the crevassed glacier for ½km. When on the glacier head towards the bottom of the gully which descends diagonally from the saddle itself. Follow this steep and often icy 40 degree gully up for 150m to the saddle. If the gully is icy some protection might be helpful.

The second way is similar but from the west. This route goes up Ringsdalen and Ringsbreen to Ringsskard as per **Hu.18**. From Ringsskard head south west under the south face of Østre Ringstind for ½km until you reach its south ridge, where Lovskard is seen for the first time; it is the most northerly, and lowest, of the three saddles on the ridge 1km to the east. At the south ridge of Østre Ringstind the glacier drops down steeply for 80m to an almost separate section in a distinct valley. It is easiest to keep closer to the south ridge of Østre Ringstind here, as opposed to the low nunatak further south. Once at the bottom of this steep crevassed section head north east across the more level glacier for ½km until the glacier rises up towards the slabs and snowfields under the west side of Lovskard. Keep well to the south of Lovskard where there is a diagonal open gully heading northwards up to the saddle. This gully, which is about 35 degrees for 80m, will be full of snow in the early summer but towards mid summer will be patchy with some easy wet scrambling sections.

The third approach to Lovskard involves the long descent from Nordre Midtmaradalstind (refer to the Dyrhaugstind pages for details on ascending this). This descent initially involves scrambling to grade III down the ridge until you approach the four pinnacles. Before the pinnacles descend a slab on the west side and pass under the pinnacles, on the west side, then regain the ridge again. Then follow the ridge down to Lovskard.

Once at Lovskard follow the ridge south east along a rise on the arête for 250m which then drops very steeply down to the saddle on the south east side of this rise. The descent to this saddle is best tackled on the loose south west side but the whole rise can also be avoided on the south west side on a series of wide sloping shelves, thus avoiding this steep descent. Continuing south east there is another rise to be negotiated. The climb out of the saddle onto this rise is initially steep and loose for 10m but eases off afterwards and is somewhat airy as it follows the arête up and down to the most south easterly saddle at the base of the north west arête of Midtmaradalstind. From this saddle the real ascent begins. It is initially quite simple to follow the arête, keeping to the south west of any obstacles until you reach a large overhanging crag called Halls hammer (not to be confused with the Halls hammer on the Skagastøls ridge). This crag is best avoided on the south west side by initially descending some 30m down a gully. Then head south along level ledges to reach a larger shelf with some vegetation on it. Follow this ledge up under an overhanging block until you get to a flatter area. Cross this flatter area and then drop down slightly to a long sloping shelf that leads up to a loose gully. The traverse between the flatter area and the loose gully along the sloping shelf involves climbing to grade III. Once in the loose gully it is easy to follow this up to the main arête again. Continue to follow the main arête south east over a gently rising section for about 100m until it levels out for 10m before climbing more steeply again. At this 10m level section there is a loose gully that descends to the south west. Do not descend down this gully if going the other way as it ends in an overhang. The route now goes up the arête for a final 100m of grade III scrambling where there are numerous steep steps to surmount. During this final 100m the more difficult scrambles can be eased by veering onto the south west face occasionally.

The time from Turtagrø to Lovskard via Bandet or Ringsskard is 4½ hours, and from Turtagrø to Lovskard via Dyrhaugs ridge is 6½. From Lovskard to the summit is 2 hours. The return journeys by the same route will be slightly shorter. If the return is being made via the prefered ascent route described above then allow 4½ hours to Stølsmaradalen cabin.

The route via Bandet over Lovskard then back to Turtagrø via Ringsskard and Ringsdalen is a classic day trip of about 10 hours in the spring on skis. Due to the steepness of the final ascent and descent at Lovskard it is only suitable for experienced parties. The ridge from Lovskard to the summit of Midtmaradalstind however is a very serious undertaking in the spring.

1.11 STØLSMARADALSTIND

Stølsmaradalstind from Ringskard saddle to the north east. The steep arete on the right descends down to Vikingskard saddle. The easiest route goes up the far south ridge on the left of the picture. The steep gully on the east side of the peaks is clearly visible.

Stølsmaradalstind, 2026m, is a two peak mountain in the remote southern half of Hurrungane. It lies at the northern end of the long Stølsmaradals ridge which rises steeply between the U shaped valleys of Stølsmaradalen and Gravdalen. On the north side of the mountain there is a steep arête.

THE ROUTE FROM MURANE SETER

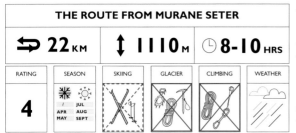

⇄ 22 KM	↕ 1110 M	⏱ 8-10 HRS

RATING	SEASON	SKIING	GLACIER	CLIMBING	WEATHER
4	❄ / JUL ☀ APR MAY AUG SEPT				

The route from Murane is the shortest and easiest. It is essentially a summer route, but possible in the spring. The final 600m up the west ridge is steep and too poorly covered in snow to be plausible to ski, especially when there is such a good alternative from Turtagrø. Murane is an old seter which lies on the east side of the road from Årdal to Turtagrø, about 4km south of the toll booth. Just to the north of the bridge over the Fardalselvi river is a turning to the east onto a flat area where there is good parking. From here pass to the north of the seter houses and over a small spur to reach the lush Austanbotnelvi stream and a wonderful view of Austanbotntind itself. Follow this stream up for a pleasant 2km, crossing over to the east bank where the going is even easier. This crossing should not be a problem, unless the river is high with snowmelt and rain. After 2km the terrain flattens out completely and the stream bed veers east away from Austanbotntind towards a distinct saddle to the south of it. Follow the stream up towards this saddle for 1km, crossing a tributary from the south to get to a small lake, Austanbotnvatnet, 1190m. Continue east, passing to the south of this small lake towards the saddle. After the lake the lush pleasant terrain continues as you climb up the gentle grassy slopes for 1km to reach Gravdalsbandet saddle. This saddle is a thoroughfare for reindeer and there still are remains of ancient reindeer pit traps.

At Gravdalsbandet the route now heads north east into the upper reaches of Gravdalen for 3km towards the mountain of Midtre Ringstind. There is a remarkable kilometre-wide level shelf heading in the same direction along the bottom of the hugely impressive east face of the Austanbotntind massif. Follow this shelf, which is largely mixed grass, rock slab and a few lingering snowfields, especially early in the summer, for the 3km passing to the west of the small knoll, 1414m, in the valley. Here the terrain starts to get somewhat awkward as more and more moraine deposits are encountered. About ½km to the south of the lake 1368m, at the end of the Gravdalen valley, there is a substantial moraine deposit. Do not venture onto this but head east along it and cross the small stream that emerges from it, to arrive at the base of the long slope up the west ridge.

This west ridge is more of a slope with a huge precipitous drop down the south side. The slope is not steep at about 25 degrees, but it is a sustained slog up boulders for two 300m sections. The first 300m section initially goes south east, keeping a few hundred metres to the north of the large drop down the south side of the ridge. In the earlier half of summer there is a broad snow filled gully which can easily be ascended, or if the snow is hard and you don't have an ice axe clamber up the slab/boulder mix to the north of the gully. As you approach the top of this 300m climb the gradient steepens and it is easiest to veer southwards towards the now huge drops down the south side of the ridge, but still keep a healthy distance. There is some easy scrambling through this steeper section to gain gentler ground again at the bottom of the next 300m section.

The final 300m climb now heads north east up a broad ridge which is covered in boulders. This grind is greatly eased by the ever present, very impressive views across Gravdalen below to Austanbotntind and Store Ringstind. It also takes a bit under an hour to ascend this second half and the easiest line to take is

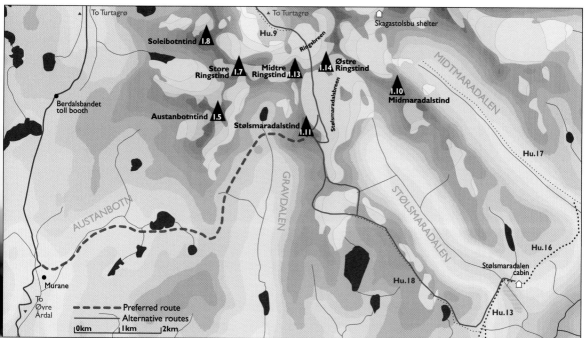

straight up the middle of the slope to the saddle between the main summit and the south top. It is only when you approach the top that the view over the majority of Hurrungane suddenly bursts forth. From this saddle there is a steep gully that descends down to the huge Stølsmaradalsbreen glacier below, which is sometimes used as an ascent route.

From the saddle there is an easy and pleasant ten minute walk across stable stones to the main summit. The return is by the same route where early in the season some snowfields will ease the descent into Gravdalen. To continue to Turtagrø requires glacial experience and equipment and the descent to Stølsmaradalen cabin is 5 hours.

Alternative Routes

There are three different locations to start an ascent of Stølsmaradalstind. Two of these are essentially summer routes, and the third, from Turtagrø hotel, is an excellent route for a spring ski ascent.

The two summer routes start from the south. The first from Murane is the simplest and is described in the preferred section above. The other route from the south is from the remote but charming Stølsmaradalen cabin via the long south ridge. It is a long way to the cabin and as such it might be better to use the cabin as a base to ascend both Midtmaradalstind and Stølsmaradalstind during the same stay. I have described this route in the next paragraph. The spring route from Turtagrø is a ski classic, crossing two large glaciers and a high pass. It is also possible to do this route over the glaciers in the summer but this is a more demanding expedition. I have described this route from Turtagrø in last paragraph in this section.

Walk to Stølsmaradalen cabin by following route **Hu.14** from Hjelle to Vetti Farm and up Brendeteigen for 4½ hours in total, or follow the routes **Hu.11** and **Hu.13** for 5 hours in total. It would be best to go one way and return the other. From the cabin cross the Stølsmaradalsøla stream and return south for 1km to the junction of the routes **Hu.13** and **Hu.14**. Near this junction there is a stream tumbling down from the west. Head up the scrub on the north side of this steam until the terrain becomes much steeper and you have to weave between outcrops. Halfway up the relentless slope the stream divides and the route continues to follow the northern side. Here try and climb up a short grassy spur just to the north of the stream to avoid the ravine which stream flows out of. At the top of this grassy spur the gradient eases and pleasant ground leads up to the south of knoll 1513m and north of

a crystal clear lake at 1425m. Continue past the lake in a north west direction and descend slightly to a saddle and then up a small and safe glacier to the large cairn 1km away on the knoll 1605m. From knoll 1605m continue north west across easy undulating bare rock for a further kilometre to knoll 1664m and then descend 1km to the edge of the glacier. If alone descend to the snout of this glacier and then climb the steep scree covered ridge to knoll 1787m. If in a party rope up and head west across this glacier to the saddle on the west side between the knolls 1700m and 1787m, and then head up to knoll 1787m for 1km on loose scree. This glacial crossing is usually crevasse free, but there are crevasses on the south side of this glacier, and conditions change annually. From knoll 1787m descend northwards for ½km to another saddle at the bottom of the final slope. Do not venture too far onto the glacier on the east of this descent as there are treacherous crevasses on this section of Stølsmaradalsbreen glacier. From this saddle, at about 1735m, the final climb to the summit starts. Initially the gradient is easy but soon steepens considerably. The steeper section is best negotiated some 50m to the west of the blunt ridge. The gradient eases off slightly for a short section, and then climbs steeply again through outcrops to the south top, 1993m. From the south top there is a simple and short descent down to a saddle and then an easy ascent along the rocky ridge to the main summit at 2026 m. The total time from Stølsmaradalen cabin is about 6 hours up and 5 returning.

The route from Turtagrø is essentially a spring ski route, and a superb one at that. The route starts at Turtagrø and follows the route **Hu.18** for 6km to Ringsskard saddle. In April and early May there is substantial snow cover on this glacier and if one is skiing it is not necessary to go roped up, but experience is necessary. In the summer a rope is essential to cross this (or any) glacier. At Ringsskard the sharp pyramid of Stølsmaradalstind appears for the first time. From Ringsskard continue to follow **Hu.18** across the almost flat Stølsmaradalsbreen glacier southwards for 2km, passing to the east of the mountain. After you have passed the summit there is a wide steep glacier filled gully that descends from between the main summit and the south top, 1993m. This gully is sometimes used as an ascent route, but it is steep, about 45 degrees, and should only be considered by experienced parties. In the spring it may be avalanche prone and in the summer it is often icy, and there is a large bergschrund at the bottom. The more usual ascent route continues south for a further ½km on the glacier passing to the east of the south top, 1993m, until you round a buttress and can climb up onto the south ridge. During the summer be wary of crevasses as you skirt round this buttress onto the scree covered south ridge. Once on the south ridge the ascent route described above can be followed to the summit. The total time in the spring on skis is about 8 hours, and about 10 hours in the summer on foot.

There is also a route up the north arête from Vikingskard. This route is five pitches with climbing up to grade IV. Vikingskard is most easily gained from Stølsmaradalsbreen glacier on the east side as opposed to the Gravdalen side.

1.12 STEINDALSNOSI

Steindalsnosi rises with grace above the frozen Prestesteinvatnet lake in the winter...

Steindalsnosi, 2025m, is the smaller sibling of Fannaråken and forms the other half of the graceful symmetry that makes the grand panorama of mountains seen from the spectacular Sognefjellsveien mountain road. It is the easiest of all the mountains in Hurrungane to ascend in the summer or spring.

THE ROUTE FROM TURTAGRØ HOTEL

⇆ 8 km	↕ 750 m	🕐 4-5 hrs

RATING	SEASON	SKIING	GLACIER	CLIMBING	WEATHER
2	JUL APR AUG MAY SEPT JUN OCT				

From Turtagrø drive towards Lom for about 8km until you pass the small Gjuvvatnet lake and come to the parking place by the sign 1300 m.o.h. (above sea level). In the summer park here and start climbing up the spur, called Gjuvvasshøgdi, on the east side of the road. Keep on the north side of the spur as you climb steeply. After some 15 minutes the gradient eases and the terrain becomes much flatter and you can see a small rise marked, 1521m, ½km away to the east. Head for this knoll. In the late spring, after the road opens, it is perhaps better to park near the dam which is another 2km further along the road to Lom. Head south from the dam for 2km to reach the same knoll 1521m, thereby avoiding the steep slope up Gjuvvasshøgdi. It should be noted that only the lower half of Steindalsnosi is suitable for skiing as the upper half is often bare.

From knoll 1521m continue east across pleasant mixed grass and slab terrain, climbing gently for a long ½km until you gain knoll 1605m. After knoll 1605m the pleasant terrain is short lived as you continue eastwards up the increasing gradient of the ridge which is soon covered in stones. It is best to keep to the north side of this

... and in the summer.

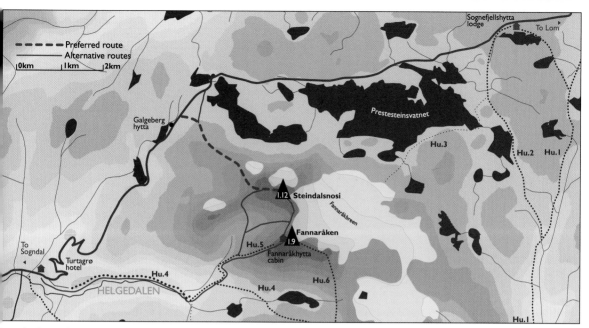

broad ridge as the gradient is more even and there is an inspiring view over Prestesteinvatnet lake and the Smørstabb massif beyond. Towards the top of the ridge the gradient steepens again slightly but is still relatively easy. After this steeper section the gradient eases considerably as you gain the summit plateau. It should take no longer than an hour from knoll 1605m to reaching the summit plateau.

Once on the summit plateau continue east across easy stones for a pleasant kilometre during which there are some excellent views, especially over to Fannaråken which seems just a stone's throw away, and Styggedals ridge beyond that. The cairn seems to be east of the summit on a separate and slightly lower hump.

Return by the same route. Otherwise descend via either of the alternative ascent routes down into Steindalen. If taking this Steindalen route you could also make an ascent of Fannaråken, possibly staying the night during the summer, or just return to Turtagrø via Helgedalen.

Alternative Routes

The simplest route up Steindalsnosi is via the north west ridge as described above. There is another, but seldom used and unmarked, route up from Steindalen from the south. This route is rough but is useful if you want to combine Steindalsnosi and Fannaråken. This is described below.

To reach Steindalen leave Turtagrø hotel and head up Helgedalen to the Ekrehytta as if you were going up Fannaråken. Continue to climb past Ekrehytta on the marked path to Fannaråken up past a steeper section for a good half an hour until the gradient levels out and you are some 100m above the Steindalen valley floor which lies steeply down to the west. This is described in more detail on the Fannaråken pages (40-41). Leave the path here, and traverse across the mixed vegetation, slab and stone slopes in a northerly direction into Steindalen itself. Keep on the bearing, trying not to lose height until the river comes up to meet you about ¾km into the valley. The terrain now begins to be dominated by stones. Continue up the stony valley for another ½km and cross over the submerged river to reach the north side. From here there is a wide bowl which leads steeply up to a saddle on the main ridge above. Clamber up the rocks and stones of the steep bowl for a good half hour to reach the saddle and a rewarding view to Breheimen in the north west. From the saddle it is a pleasant 1km walk to the north east across a shallow slope to reach the summit. From Turtagrø allow four hours to the summit, of which two hours are after leaving the path above the Ekrehytta. Return by the same route or descend the north west ridge as described above.

It is also possible to continue further up the Steindalen valley to the saddle between Steindalsnosi and Fannaråken. At this saddle is an open view over the huge Fannaråkbreen glacier, which incidentally is a superb ski descent in the spring down to Sognefjellshytta lodge. From this saddle there is a steep scramble up the boulders on the ridge to the north for 100m of vertical ascent to gain a more gentle but still stony ridge. This more gentle ridge then veers north west for ½km to reach the summit.

Looking up the north west ridge of Steindalsnosi from knoll 1605m.

1.13 MIDTRE RINGSTIND

Midtre Ringstind dominates the view southwards down Ringsdalen. The ridge on the left is the east ridge and the easier west ridge is on the right.

Midtre Ringstind, 2025m, is a pyramid that rises up from the glaciers at the end of Ringsdalen. There are three ridges that lead down to three saddles and then up to neighbouring mountains. Due to its popular neighbour, Store Ringstind, it is seldom climbed, but the two mountains can easily be combined in a day.

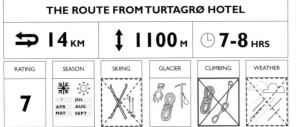

THE ROUTE FROM TURTAGRØ HOTEL		
⮀ 14 KM	↕ 1100 M	🕐 7-8 HRS

RATING	SEASON	SKIING	GLACIER	CLIMBING	WEATHER
7					

From Turtagrø drive 3km on the small road to Årdal until there is a small rough gravel road heading south up Ringsdalen for ½km. Park here and head down to the river, cross the dam, and head up Ringsdalen and onto Ringsbreen glacier as described on route **Hu.6** and on the Store Ringstind pages (36-37). The route goes up Ringsdalen for 5km and then steeply up the rock band on the east side of the valley. Once at the top of this rock band head south for ½km to the edge of Ringsbreen glacier. At the edge of the glacier, rope up and head up to Gravdalskard across the Ringsbreen glacier to the north of Midtre Ringstind, as described on the Store Ringstind pages.

Looking down the glaciated east face of Store Ringstind. At the bottom of the slope is Gravdalskard, beyond which is Midtre Ringstind. Storen dominates the skyline on the left.

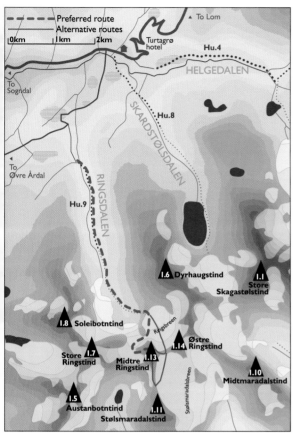

Alternative Routes

There are three routes up to the summit and each of them follows one of the three ridges. The south ridge from Vikingskard is the most difficult and involves six pitches of climbing with a section of grade VI and much at grade IV. I have not described this route. There is another route up the east ridge from Ringsskard saddle and this apparently involves some climbing to grade III. I have not described this route either but it looks harder than the grade III suggested. The easiest route is up the west ridge from Gravdalskard and only involves scrambling, and this is described as the preferred route.

Midtre Ringstind is a very difficult mountain to do solo, as it is pretty much entirely surrounded by glacier. During the spring it is possible to get to Gravdalskard on skis un-roped, but, the ascent up the easiest west ridge will be steep and difficult, although within the scope of experienced mountaineers, given good conditions.

Gravdalskard itself is a crevassed saddle with Ringsbreen on one side and Gravdalsbreen on the other. On the east side of this saddle the west ridge of Midtre Ringstind plunges into the ice. Clamber up the slabs at the bottom of the ridge and then up the loose boulders and scree for ¼ hour until the gradient starts to steepen. When it steepens, try and be some 30m to the south of the main ridge line. Here there is a vague route up some shallow corners for another ¼ hour until the ground levels off again. One of these corners is grade II for about 10m but this could be slightly more difficult in the wet as there are heavy lichen growths on the rock of this seldom visited peak. Once past this steeper section the route eases off and climbs an easy slope of boulders and bare slabs to the summit. This easier final section also continues some 20-40m to the south of the ridge for another ¼ hour until the small cairn is reached.

From left Store, Midtre and Østre Ringstind from Midtmaradals ridge.

The return is by the same route; however, extra care must be taken due to the slippery rocks if wet when descending the west ridge. It is usual to combine this mountain with Store Ringstind and if doing so allow three extra hours to climb it and return to Gravdalskard saddle before heading down to Ringsdalen again.

Skiing across Stølsmaradalsbreen towards Ringsskard, with the east ridge of Midtre Ringstind looming above.

1.14 ØSTRE RINGSTIND

Østre Ringstind from the northern end of Ringsbreen. The ridge on the left is the east ridge and the saddle with Nordre Midtmaradalstind, while the ridge on the right is the west ridge at the bottom of which is the Ringsskard saddle.

Østre Ringstind, 2002m, is another a pyramid that rises up from the glaciers at the end of Ringsdalen. There are three ridges on it, two of which descend into glaciers while the third descends steeply to a saddle and then a neighbouring top. It is a seldom visited peak, being somewhat overlooked by its higher neighbours.

THE ROUTE FROM TURTAGRØ HOTEL

⇆ 15 KM	↕ 1020 M	⏲ 7-8 HRS

RATING	SEASON	SKIING	GLACIER	CLIMBING	WEATHER
7	❄ ☀ / JUL APR AUG MAY SEPT				

From Turtagrø hotel drive the 3km on the Årdal road to the gravel track. Park here and follow the route **Hu.9** up Ringsdalen to the northern edge of the Ringsbreen glacier as described on the Store Ringstind pages (36-37).

Østre Ringstind from Stølsmaradalstind to the south. The ridge on the left is the west ridge.

At the edge of the glacier rope up and head south up to Ringsskard saddle. This is a relatively gentle glacial crossing of about 1km. At the bottom there are some streams which have carved deep slots, and there might also be some small moulins (wells). As you ascend keep to the obvious line up the middle of the glacier as this is relatively (but not entirely) crevasse free. At the saddle there is just a narrow band of flat easy slab to cross to get onto the Stølsmaradalsbreen saddle. The west ridge goes up from here.

From the saddle head east along the top of the glacier below the mountain for about 300m until there is a ramp of snow heading diagonally up the mountain above a small isolated outcrop. Follow this ramp up, still heading east for another 50m until the rock above becomes easier to ascend. Now head straight up the mountain to reach an isolated snowfield which persists until the mid summer at least. Climb some 100 vertical metres up this snowfield, which is about 35 degrees, until you reach the top of it. An ice axe could be essential here. Do not stray too far to the east at the top of the snowfield as the rock over there is mostly slippery slab formations. Instead scramble straight up some corners for another 50 vertical metres until the gradient eases as you approach the top. Suddenly, as you reach the top, the awesome view eastwards over Skagastølstind and Styggedalstind bursts forth.

It is much easier in the spring to ski to the Ringsskard saddle than it is in the summertime to walk there. However, the conditions on the south west face might thwart any attempt to climb it without additional equipment. Crampons and protection are recommended as some sections towards the top are steep and a slip could be fatal.

The return is by the same route to Ringsskard. It is a tall order to continue on and do the other two Ringstind mountains in a day, but it is sometimes done. Unless you are proficient climbers willing

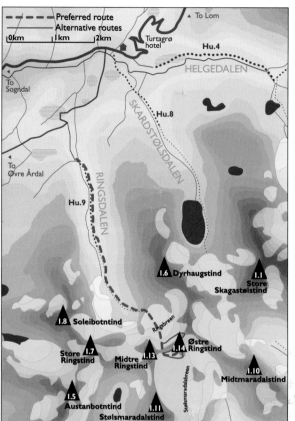

to tackle the east ridge of Midtre Ringstind then it is necessary to skirt round the north side of Midtre Ringstind to Gravdalskard. This skirting round under the north side of Midtre Ringstind is steep, crevassed and also exposed to stones rolling down the ice. An ice axe, crampons, rope, rescue pulleys and experience are the minimum requirements here. Once at Gravdalskard the route up Midtre and Store Ringstind are as described on pages (48-49 and 36-37). To do either of the other two mountains add 2 ½ hours for each.

Alternative Routes

There are four routes up to the summit, one up each of the thre ridges, all of which are climbs. The fourth and easiest is up the south west face, which is a scramble and is described above in the prefered route section.

Of the three ridges the most remote is the north east ridge. This ridge rises from the saddle with the top to Nordre Midtmaradalstind and can be gained after a long and demanding traverse from Turtagrø hotel over Dyrhaugstind. See the Dyrhaugstind pages for further details. This saddle can also be gained with great difficulty from Ringsbreen glacier to the north, or with some difficulty from Stølsmaradalsbreen glacier to the south. Either of these ascents from the glacier to the saddle involves two pitches up loose slabs with climbing up to grade III and possibly a bergschrund also, especially in the late summer. From the saddle the ridge is obvious and looms above you. It is five exposed pitches with climbing up to grade IV, and much at of it at grade III.

The west ridge and the south ridge both start from the vicinity of Ringsskard saddle, one directly from the saddle and the other from ½km to the south east of it. They are both up to grade III, with much of these ridges at grade II. The south ridge is a more slabby character while the west ridge has more broken corners, and both require protection. Between these ridges is the south west face (described above as preferred route), which is grade II and doesn't need protection in good dry conditions.

The steep west ridge of Østre Ringstind is harder than the south face, which is to the right of the picture.

MAMMALS OF HURRUNGANE

In the winter Hurrungane is a harsh environment. Consequently there is not a rich mammal presence. Even in the surrounding valleys, where there is some protection and under the snow some food, life is a struggle for most. However, in the summer conditions are kind and most mammals, especially the herbivores, flourish.

Key to how the carnivores flourish and breed is how the small rodents, like lemmings and voles breed. About every 3-5 years there is a population explosion or lemming year. It is thought that after such a year, the plants which have sustained the small rodents and been severely gnawed produce unpalatable chemicals which hinder the rodents' digestion. These chemicals only last a few years in the plants and are then weak enough for the rodents to feast again.

In lemming years many carnivores and birds of prey maximize their breeding. Indeed, some can only breed successfully in such years. The resulting abundance of predators the following year also hinders any small rodent population explosion and the population wanes again.

Ursus arctos, Bear, Bjørn. 225cm. An extremely rare migrant which was resident in Utladalen in the first half of last century. Bears are now just found in the remote coniferous forests to the east of the watershed. Very occasionally one migrates westwards but it is very unlikely one would get as far as Hurrungane. During the summer bears prefer the higher forests and in the winter they hibernate in a cave or hole. They eat berries, insects and carrion, but will sometimes kill large mammals, especially in the spring. Can live for up to 35 years.

Alopex lagopus, Arctic Fox, Fjellrev. 65cm. In the early half of the last century they were rare in Hurrungane. Now they are threatened in Scandinavia, despite protection. This demise is due to increased competition from red foxes and climate warming. The arctic fox is found in a few isolated pockets of open moorland, mostly much further north, but one pocket is nearby. They survive off lemmings, voles, ptarmigan, and carrion. They live in extensive underground dens. Both sexes turn white in winter. They live up to 10 years.

Gulo gulo, Wolverine, Jerv. 65cm. A rare resident of the high forest and tundra areas in the mountains. They were heavily persecuted, to virtual eradication, but are reappearing in the vicinity after becoming protected in 1973. They hunt reindeer and rodents, and rarely sheep. They are considered to kill wantonly but cache food for leaner periods. They live in extensive dens in winter, often in a snowdrift. In early summer the female and young often move to another den. The sexes are alike, but the male is bigger. They can live up to 12 years.

Mustela ermina, Stoat, Røyskatt. 30cm. They are a fairly common resident throughout Hurrungane from the mature forests up to the tundra, especially around the tree line. They hunt small rodents and birds, including grouse, and will even kill a hare. They also eat carrion. They live in fur lined dens in burrows, rock crevices or tree hollows. The sexes are alike but the male is bigger. In the summer they are brown and yellowish white, but in winter all white. The tip of the tail remains black throughout. They can live for up to 4 years.

Lynx lynx, Lynx, Gaupe. 110cm. The lynx was an uncommon resident in Hurrungane in the earlier half of the last century, but has now been eradicated. Occasionally migrants from the east of Norway's main watershed may establish a territory but they will soon be persecuted to move on. They are at home in remote, rocky, mature forests with an undergrowth. They hunt mammals and birds and will also take livestock. They make a den in caves or under an overhang. They do not hibernate. Lynx can live up to 15 years.

Vulpes vulpes, Red Fox, Rev. 75cm. A common, but shy, resident of the valleys surrounding the mountains. They tend to keep in the forests or scrub but may venture onto the tundra. It is the only carnivorous mammal whose numbers are increasing, mostly at the expense of the arctic fox. They hunt small rodents, like voles, but will also eat insects, berries, birds, eggs and many other things if hungry. They live in extensive multi-roomed lairs dug in the earth. The sexes are alike. In the wild they can live up to 9 years.

Martes martes, Pine Marten, Mår. 55cm. They are found in the mature forests, especially the coniferous areas, that surround the mountains. These residents are not rare but are seldom seen as they prefer to be nocturnal, and if active by day are shy. They hunt small rodents, especially voles, but also eat squirrels, birds, eggs and berries. Their preferred den is a hole in a tree, especially old squirrel dreys, but they will also use rock crevices which they line with moss. The sexes are alike, but the males are slightly bigger. They can live up to 10 years.

Mustela nivalis ssp. nivalis, Least Weasel, Snømus. 20cm. Like the stoat, they are fairly common residents throughout Hurrungane, but venture higher up the mountains. They are more specialized to hunt small rodents than the stoat and chase them down their burrows or under snow. They will also hunt small birds. Like the stoat they cache food. They live in fur lined burrows in the ground or between rocks. Similar colourings to the stoat in summer and winter, but never a black tip to tail. The females are smaller. They can live up to 3 years.

***Alces alces*, Elk, Elg. 270cm.** Elk are unusual and rare residents in the wooded valleys which surround the mountains. Elk are much more common to the east of the main watershed in Norway. They are generally found in the mature forests up to the tree line, and favour marshy areas. Despite being up to 700kg they can subsist on shoots, twigs and bark of trees, supplemented in the summer with plants, leaves and aquatic plants. They are excellent swimmers. They do not have dens but rest in the forest. They can live for up to 25 years.

***Rangifer tarandus*, Reindeer, Rein. 200cm.** These resident reindeer are feral descendents of the tame herds released to replace the original wild herd, which vanished in the early half of the last century from Hurrungane. The remnants of this wild herd are now just found in the Dovre/Rondane areas. In Hurrungane they are found in the remoter southern valleys, namely Gravdalen. They eat lichens, especially *Cladonia rangiferina* (see page 61), grass, sedges, shoots and fungi. Both sexes have antlers. They are very gregarious. They can live for 12 years.

***Cervus elaphus*, Red Deer, Hjort. 200cm.** These residents are found in the wooded valleys surrounding the massif. Once rare, they are becoming widespread in the mature and mountain birch forests. They graze on shoots, bark, heather, grasses and sedges. Hinds and their young tend to be gregarious while stags are more peripheral, except in the rutting season when mature males acquire and guard a harem. They do not have dens but rest at feeding areas. The males are larger and have antlers. They can live for about 15 years.

***Capreolus capreolus*, Roe Deer, Rådyr. 110cm.** They are unusual residents of the lower forested valleys surrounding the massif near the cultivated areas. They sometimes succumb to harsh winters, to which they are not as well adapted as red deer. They are selective in their diet and choose the best morsels. These include young leaves, herbs, grasses, heather, berry bushes, fungi and shoots depending on the season. They are usually solitary and territorial. The sexes are similar but the male larger. They can live for up to 10 years.

***Sciurus vulgaris*, Red Squirrel, Ekorn. 20cm.** A common resident in the forested valleys around the massif and found down to farmed areas. They live in coniferous woodlands and eat pine and spruce seeds from the cones. They also eat nuts, bark, fungi, berries and sometimes bird eggs and young. They store food when available to help them through the winter. They nest in dreys, which are 30cm spheres of twigs and moss built up trees. They do not hibernate. The sexes are alike but the female chases males at breeding. They can live for 5 years.

***Lepus timidus*, Mountain Hare, Hare. 55cm.** A common resident found from the mountain birch forest to the upper limit of vegetation. They eat grasses, herbs and shoots in summer, while in winter they browse heather, berries and various scrub. They are mainly nocturnal and during the day remain in a form, a shallow burrow which is usually open and hidden under scrub or rock. In bad winter weather they burrow in snow. They are generally solitary animals. The sexes are alike and turn white in winter. They can live for 7 years.

***Lemnus lemmus*, Lemming, Lemen. 12cm.** A quite common resident of the mountain birch and tundra zones, which can become very widespread and abundant in a lemming year. They can have 10 young per litter and 6 litters per summer. They reach sexual maturity after 2 weeks, so if conditions are good they can reach huge numbers. This roughly happens every 4 years. They eat grasses and mosses. They live in burrows under stones in summer and large tunnel systems below the snow in winter. The sexes are alike. They can live up to 2 years.

***Sorex araneus*, Common Shrew, Vanlig Spissmus. 7cm.** Quite common in the wooded valleys around Hurrungane, but rarely seen. They seldom leave cover and spend most of the time in thick grass, scrub or bracken. Their nest of grass is in a small burrow, often under a tussock or log. In winter they are underground most of the time. They eat worms, slugs, insects and woodlice. They are solitary and aggressive except during the breeding season. They are good swimmers. They can live up to 2 years, but few reach a year.

***Microtus agrestis*, Field Vole, Markmus. 10cm.** Quite common in the forested valleys around Hurrungane. They prefer grassy woods and meadows. In summer they eat grasses and herbs, but in winter may gnaw bark from trees. Their nest is a sphere of grass, usually under a tussock. This nest is on a network of surface runways and underground tunnels. Population explosions in some years similar to the lemming. Females are more social than males, otherwise the sexes are alike. They can live for 2 years, but seldom pass a year.

***Microtus oeconomus*, Tundra Vole, Fjellrotte. 13cm.** Quite common in the higher forests and moorland zones. They prefer more swampy areas than the field vole and live higher up. They eat sedges and other aquatic plants. In winter they eat the roots of these plants. Their nests is a sphere of grasses and moss above the ground in swampy areas, otherwise they nest in an extensive tunnel system. They have similar population explosions to the lemming and field vole, every 3-5 years. The sexes are alike. They can live for 2 years, but usually survive less than 1.

BIRDS OF HURRUNGANE

Hurrungane has a rich and diverse birdlife in the summer. The birds found can roughly be divided in four main groups, or taxomic orders: *Passeriformes* (perching and songbirds, pages 54-56), *Charadriiformes* (waders etc. pages 56-57), *Galliformes* (grouse etc. page 57) and *Falconiformes* (birds of prey, page 58). There are also some others.

The *Passeriformes*, pages 54-56, tend to be summer visitors which arrive to take advantage of the abundance of insects. With this almost limitless supply of food they can easily raise at least one brood. These birds are very numerous and tend to be found mainly in the upper aboreal zone (mountain birch and the willow scrub zones) from about 500m altitude up to 1200m. Most of these *Passeriformes* will migrate to warmer climates for the winter.

The waders of the *Charadriiformes* order, pages 56-57, similarly arrive as summer visitors to take advantage of the abundant insect diet on which they can rear a brood. They are also in the upper aboral

zone and the moorland zone. They are usually by water within these zones, notably lakes, marshes and streams. Likewise they migrate to escape the harsh winter which they cannot survive.

The *Galliformes*, page 57, are resident. They are mainly vegetarian and live off buds, shoots and seeds. As the summer unfolds they also eat many of the berries available. These berries also sustain them throughout the harsh winter. The willow grouse and ptarmigan are by far the commonest of these birds and form an intergral link in the winter food chain for resident birds of prey and foxes.

The *Falconiformes*, page 58, include both residents and summer visitors. These birds of prey generally live in the upper aboreal and moorland zones breeding on cliff ledges. These birds prey on the influx of smaller summer visitors and rodents to sutain their breeding, and the *Galliformes* birds or carrion to survive the winter.

Phylloscopus trochilus, **Willow Warbler, Løvsanger. 11cm.** A common summer visitor which is found in large numbers in the birch forests and the willow belt above that. It is an active and restless bird constantly darting from bush to bush looking for insects and their larvae. They nest on the ground, usually in a domed grass and leaf nest beside a hummock. Almost identical to the chiffchaff, but has darker legs.

Hippolais icterina, **Icterine Warbler, Gulsanger. 13cm.** A more seldom summer visitor. It is much more arboreal than the willow warbler and only occasionally ventures out of mature deciduous woodland. It is much less active than the willow warbler also. Only likely to be seen in surrounding valleys. They nest in shrubs, hedges and thickets.

Sylvia atricapilla, **Blackcap, Munk. 14cm.** A more seldom summer visitor. Arboreal in nature, they are mostly found in deciduous and mixed forests where there is significant undergrowth. They build a cuplike nest of grasses in bushes. They feed off insects and larvae but also consume most berries when available. The female has a brown, not black, cap. Their song is considered to one of the most beautiful of all birdsong.

Sylvia communis, **Whitethroat, Tornsanger. 14cm.** A common summer visitor, found in lower arboreal regions of the valleys where there is thick undergrowth, but absent from higher ground. A very active bird darting in and out of cover. Eats insects, larvae, ants and fruits and berries. Nests in dense vegetation near the ground, the male building several rough nests from which the female chooses.

Regulus regulus, **Goldcrest, Fuglekonge. 9cm.** The smallest European bird is an infequent resident around Hurrungane. Found only in the surrounding valleys, predominantly in conifer forests. Feeds on insects, larvae and insect eggs. The nest, built by both members from mosses and spiders' webs, is basket shaped and hangs from conifer branches. In winter it frequents deciduous forests and undergrowth.

Parus montanus, **Willow Tit, Granmeis. 11cm.** A common resident in the woods of the surrounding valleys but rare in the higher scrub and absent from the high mountains. Prefers damper locations in any woodland where there are rotten trees in which the female can excavate a nesting hole. It subsists on insects, spiders and some berries.

Carduelis spinus, **Siskin, Grønnsisik. 11cm.** A common resident found in the valleys but venturing up to the highest conifers in the summer. In the winter it retreats to the deciduous valleys, to the alders and birch. The nest is usually high up in conifer trees and is a small cup of twigs. The siskin eats tree seeds, predominantly conifers in the summer and alder in the winter. Often in flocks, sometimes mixed with redpoll flocks.

Carduelis flammea, **Redpoll, Gråsisik. 13cm.** A common resident in the higher reaches of the valleys in the mountain birch and willow shrub zones. They are gregarious birds often seen in small mobile flocks. In winter they retreat to the lower deciduous woods, especially alder. Their food is mixed but includes birch and alder seeds. Nests in trees and bushes, sometimes quite high up. The male in summer has a wash of red on its chest.

Fringilla montifringilla, Brambling, Bjørkfink. 15cm. A very common summer visitor which is usually found in the higher forests, notably in the mountain birch and willow scrub zones. They nest in trees, often near the ground in cup shaped moss and grass constructions. Their summer food tends to be insects and their larvae, predominantly moths. They are very gregarious birds, sometimes forming large flocks.

Oenanthe oenanthe, Wheatear, Steinskvett. 15cm. A common summer visitor found throughout the mountains, especially in open, stony moorlands. They are active birds always on the move. They nest in holes in the ground or walls, and the nest is a cuplike grass construction. In the summer they subsist off insects and their larvae, especially spiders. Female birds have a brown back in contrast to the steel grey of the male.

Luscinia svecica, Bluethroat, Blåstrupe. 14cm. A fairly common summer visitor. They are shy birds, but usually seen in the mountain birch and willow scrub zones, especially marshy areas. Their nests are concealed and close to the ground. Their food is insects and sometimes worms and berries. The female lacks the blue markings on the throat, which is pale instead and without the red spot.

Motacilla alba, White Wagtail, Linerle. 18cm. A common visitor to the mountain birch and willow scrub zones. An early spring arrival, it picks insects off snowfields. In the summer they subsist on insects picked off the ground. They are fast runners and dart over the ground quickly in search insects. They nest in holes and ledges just above the ground, which are lined by the females with moss, grass and feathers.

Calcarius lapponicus, Lapland Bunting, Lappspurv. 15cm. A summer visitor found in the willow scrub zone and the open, rocky moorland above it. Their nests are placed on the ground against a hummock and made of grass. They subsist on insects and their larvae picked off the ground while darting about. The birds can be gregarious, especially outside the breeding season. Females lack the black chest and face.

Emberiza citrinella, Yellowhammer, Gulspurv. 17cm. An uncommon resident of the wooded valleys surrounding the mountains, especially in clearings and cultivated land. The nest is a cup of grass near or on the ground at the base of a bush. They eat insects, seeds and berries. Outside the breeding season they are quite gregarious and form flocks. The female is quite similar to the male but a paler yellow colour.

Pyrrhula pyrrhula, Bullfinch, Dompap. 17cm. An uncommon resident of the valleys where it is found in mixed woods and scrub, usually near cultivation. It is absent from the willow scrub zone upwards and rare in the mountain birch zone. They feed on seeds, buds and fruits and sometimes moths and other insects. They are shy, seldom leave cover or form flocks, but are often seen in pairs.

Saxicola rubetra, Whinchat, Buskskvett. 13cm. A common summer visitor seen frequently in the higher arboreal zones up to the willow scrub and the open moorland above it. The nest, constructed by the female, is on the ground hidden amongst the grass or under a bush, and made of grass and lined with moss. Their food is insects and their larvae and sometimes worms. Often seen perching upright on a small bush.

Anthus pratensis, Meadow Pipit, Heipiplerke. 15cm. A very common summer visitor found in the upper aboreal zone to the alpine vegetation zone. Its neat cuplike grassy nest is found on the ground hidden amongst grass or heather clumps. Often seen making short flights, rising and returning to the ground while looking for its food which consists of insects and sometimes worms and seeds. The female is similar to the male.

Emberiza schoeniclus, Reed Bunting, Sivspurv. 15cm. A summer visitor occasionally spotted by marshy areas, especially if there are reedbeds nearby. They eat seeds and cereals, but will also eat insects and their larvae. The female builds a cup shaped nest on the ground or in a bush from grass and lines it with plant down. The female is brown and has a brown moustache and also lacks the black head and chest markings of the male.

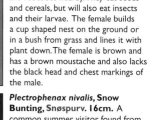

Plectrophenax nivalis, Snow Bunting, Snøspurv. 16cm. A common summer visitor found from the upper edge of the moorland right up the mountain tops. The nest is hidden in rock crevices and is constructed of grass and moss, then feather lined. They subsist on insects, especially flies and caddies found on snowfields. They are gregarious birds often found in small flocks. Females are a speckled brown and sandy colour.

Cinclus cinclus, Dipper, Fossekall. 18cm. A common resident beside fast flowing mountain streams and down by fast rivers in the forests. The cup shaped nest built by both sexes is near water, on a bank or behind a waterfall. It is made of grass and moss with an overhanging moss canopy. The dipper swims and dives for aquatic insects and larvae and also very small fish. Both sexes are alike. The dipper is the National Bird of Norway.

Troglodytes troglodytes, Wren, Gjerdesmett. 10cm. A familiar resident which occupies a wide habitat from cultivated land throughout the forests and into the alpine vegetation zone. The cuplike nest is built by the male from whatever is to hand and hidden in rock crevices or treeholes and is then lined by the females. They subsist off insects, especially moth larvae when available. Males and females are alike.

Eremophila alpestris, Horned Lark, Fjellerke. 17cm. A common, but seldom seen, summer visitor found in the alpine and tundra zones. The nest is a grass cup built on the open ground beside a stone. They eat insects and their larvae and also seeds, shuffling along and picking them up from the ground and off low vegetation. The horns on the head of the lark are tufts of black feathers and are more prominent in the male.

Turdus iliacus, Redwing, Rødvingetrost. 21cm. A common resident found in the aboreal zone, especially the mountain birch zone, where they are often seen darting through the trees. The nest is built by the female of grass and earth in a bush or the root plate of a fallen tree. Their food is insects, worms, slugs and berries. Outside the breeding season they are quite gregarious. Both male and females are alike.

Turdus pilaris, Fieldfare, Gråtrost. 25cm. A common resident throughout the arboreal and willow scrub zones, especially in marshy areas. They are gregarious birds and often nest in colonies among birches or pines. Their nests are constructed from grass and mud in trees. They live off insects and worms, and in the autumn berries. The digested remains of blue berries often splatter stones. The male and female are alike.

Turdus merula, Blackbird, Svarttrost. 25cm. A familar resident found throughout the aboreal zone but not the willow scrub zone. They nest in trees, often using an old nest as a base. The nest is made from grass and mud by the female. They eat a wide variety of insects and worms, but prefer fruit and berries when available. Blackbirds are quite territorial. Males are black, females a warm brown. Very rarely a partly or wholly albino one is seen.

Perisoreus infaustus, Siberian Jay, Lavskrike. 28cm. A rare, but approachable and curious, resident in the higher conifer forests around the mountains. They usually nest in pine trees preferably adorned with beard lichen. They eat pine seeds, insects and berries and store excess foods by glueing bits together with saliva and hiding them under bark for the winter. They will also take sandwich scraps. The male and female are alike.

Cuculus canorus, Cuckoo, Gjøk. 33cm. A fascinating summer visitor which is found in higher aboreal zones. The polyandrous female lays up to 20 eggs, all in different nests, particularly in meadow pipits' nests. After hatching the young cookoo ejects the other eggs and young from the nest, and receives all the food its foster parents bring, until it is three times their size. The adults are usually alike and eat any insects, even hairy caterpillars.

Corvus corax, Raven, Ravn. 64cm. A hardy resident that is usual from the upper aboreal zone to the summits. Their huge nests are made of twigs and mud, then lined with grass. These nests are on ledges, often with an overhang, or rarely in trees. They are very acrobatic flyers. Usually single or in pairs and seldom gregarious. They eat carrion, small mammals, other birds' eggs and young birds, insects and large seeds. The male and female are alike.

Dendrocopos major, Great Spotted Woodpecker, Flaggspett. 23cm. A common resident in forests surrounding the mountains. The nest is excavated in a tree by both sexes. They eat the larvae of wood-boring insects which they probe for under the bark. Occasionally they take the young and eggs of other hole nesting birds. The female lacks the red spot on the back of the head but is otherwise alike. Other woodpeckers may also be seen.

Stercorarius longicaudus, Long-tailed Skua, Fjelljo. 53cm. A summer visitor to the moorland and tundra zones, common if it is a lemming year, otherwise rare. The nest is on the ground and is aggressively defended. They hover while hunting for lemmings and other small rodents which they need to rear their young. If it is a poor lemming year they may not breed in the mountains. The male and female are similar.

Philomachus pugnax, Ruff, Brushane. 28cm. An uncommon visitor to marshy areas in the moorland zone. After a lek (dance like play) the female chooses a male, mates and then makes a nest amongst the grasses. They eat insects and their larvae during the summer. The males' ruffs have a collar of feathers to display during the lek with which to attract the females, also called reeves. Females lack this collar and are slightly darker and smaller.

Tringa hypoleucos, Common Sandpiper, Strandsnipe. 20cm. A common summer visitor, frequently seen beside mountain lakes and high mountain streams. They nest on the ground, often in a shingle hollow lined with vegetation. They feed on insects and their larvae. They are mostly solitary birds but may band into small flocks. During flight the wings are held swiftly downwards, and when static it bobs its tail continuously.

Calidris alpina, **Dunlin, Myrsnipe. 18cm.** A common summer visitor which breeds on open moorland, especially beside water or marshland. They are gregarious birds with several pairs nesting in close proximity. The nest is hidden in clumps and is lined with grass. They feed on terrestrial and aquatic insects and their larvae. Distinguished from other waders by its dark upper rump and in summer by a black belly. The sexes are alike.

Scolopax rusticola, **Woodcock, Rugde. 36cm.** A more seldom summer visitor which is found in damp, mature deciduous woodlands in the valleys around the mountains. They nest in a simple hollow at the base of a tree among dry leaves. They subsist off earthworms and insects, but also some seeds. They are seldom seen as they are predominantly nocturnal. They are usually solitary. The sexes are similar.

Charadrius hiaticula, **Ringed Plover, Sandlo. 18cm.** A common visitor to the moorland zone where it is seen along lake shores and mountain streams. The nest is a rudimentary scrape in shingle with little lining. It eats insects and their larvae. Outside the breeding season they are somewhat gregarious. The male and female are alike.

Charadrius morinellus, **Dotterel, Boltit. 23cm.** An alpine summer visitor found in the alpine zone. The nest is a scrape lined with moss and lichen. The female is the dominant sex and once the eggs are laid the male continues the domestic duties. They eat insects and their larvae. The slightly larger females are gregarious in the breeding season and both are outside it. The males feign injury if the nest is approached in the breeding season.

Lagopus mutus, **Ptarmigan, Fjellrype. 36cm.** A common resident to the alpine zone above the tree line. The nest is hidden in alpine vegetation and lined with grass and lichen. It eats shoots and berries of moorland and tundra plants. In the winter it is white but in the summer mottled, but with a more grey specking than the willow grouse. Male and female differ in degrees of mottling. Like the willow grouse it is gregarious in winter time.

Tetrao urogallus, **Capercaillie, Storfugl. 75cm.** An uncommon resident in the pine forests in the valleys surrounding the mountains. As with the black grouse the males lek in the spring, then the females nest on the ground and are solely responsible for the rearing. The males can be aggressive during this lek. They eat the shoots and buds of pine trees and also berries and seeds from many plants. The much smaller females are brown.

Gallinago gallinago, **Snipe, Enkeltbekkasin. 25cm.** A quite common summer visitor which is seen in higher marshes. Snipe may be seen rising and diving around their territory in a display, but when flushed they zigzag away rapidly. They nest in tussocks of grass in a well lined depression and lay 3-4 eggs. They eat insects and worms, if present, which they probe out of the ground with long beaks. Gregarious outside the breeding season.

Numenius arquata, **Curlew, Storspove. 56cm.** Arrives in the summer as a rare visitor from the coast to breed in the moorland zone. It nests in hollows on the ground and eats insects, berries and grass seeds. They are seldom seen around Hurrungane as it is not their preferred habitat, which is estuaries. The male and female are alike.

Pluvialis apricaria, **Golden Plover, Heilo. 23cm.** A summer visitor found in the moorland zone, especially in grassy areas, where it is quite common. They nest on the ground amongst vegetation in a scraped earth bowl. They eat insects and vegetation as well as some berries and grass seeds. They are often found in large flocks outside the breeding season. The sexes are alike.

Lagopus lagapus, **Willow Grouse, Lirype. 41cm.** A common resident found in the mountain birch and willow scrub zones. Nests in a scrape well hidden in the scrub. It eats buds, flowers and seeds of willow scrub, also berries when available. In addition it will eat some insects. Difficult to tell from ptarmigan but lives lower down the mountains and is larger. It is also white in winter and mottled in the summer with a rufus speckling.

Tetrao tetrix, **Black Grouse, Orrfugl. 48cm.** An uncommon resident in the forested valleys around the mountains, especially the higher birch forests with clearings. The males lek in spring and then the females nest on the ground hidden among vegetation. The males do not help with the young. They eat buds and shoots and also a wide variety of berries. The larger males are black but the females are a grey brown colour.

Clangula hyemalis, **Long-tailed Duck, Havella. 50cm.** An uncommon summer visitor from the coast, it comes to moorland lakes to breed in the summer. The nest is a hidden hollow among vegetation and lined with down. In the summer it eats aquatic insects and also some berries and plants. Only the male (drake) has the long tail feathers and the female is, as in many ducks, brown and undistinctive. They are fast flyers.

Gavia stellata, Red-throated Diver, Smålom. 46cm. A summer visitor to small high lakes at, or above, the tree line during the breeding period in the summer. The nest is usually on an island or point and is constructed from a mound of available vegetation. They feed off small fish which they dive for, often on a larger nearby lake. They can remain submerged for a minute. The sexes are alike and have a red throat patch in the summer only.

Gavia arctica, Black-throated Diver, Storlom. 64cm. A summer visitor to high moorland lakes at, or above, the tree line. They prefer to nest on an island or skerry. The nest is a spartan mound of available vegetation. They feed on fish, for which they can dive up to two minutes. They tend to occupy larger lakes than the red-throated diver. The sexes are alike and have a black throat in the summer only. In the winter the plumage is plainer.

Falco columbarius, Merlin, Dvergfalk. 30cm. An uncommon summer visitor to the mountain birch, willow scrub and moorland zones. Nests in trees in old raven nests or on rocky ledges. They eat small birds, notably meadow pipits. They will also take, but are not dependent, on small rodents. The male has a blue-grey back and crown while the female, which is the same size, has a brown crown and back. It is very fast.

Falco peregrinus, Peregrine Falcon, Vandrefalk. 48cm. A rarer sight than the merlin, this resident falcon is found in the upper arboreal and mountain birch zones where there are cliffs. They nest on a ledge year after year. They feed on medium sized birds which they swoop on and kill mid-air with a blow from their back toe. Usually solitary. The female is larger than the male and slightly darker. They can fly at a terrific speed.

Falco rusticolus, Gyrfalcon, Jaktfalk. 60cm. A rare resident of the moorland zone. Their nests are old raven or eagle nests on cliff ledges, or are scrapes on a ledge, preferably with a view of their hunting grounds. Their prey is often willow grouse or ptarmigan, but they will also take small mammals. They hunt by flying low over the ground but will sometimes soar. Their breeding success depends on the amount of prey for that year.

Accipiter nisus, Sparrowhawk, Spurvehauk. 36cm. An uncommon resident of the wooded valleys around the mountains. Their nests are untidy masses of old twigs lined with fresh leafy ones, usually in a pine tree. Both parents hunt for the chicks during breeding. They hunt small woodland birds by flying very fast along the margins of woodland clearings near the ground. The female is larger and darker than the male.

Accipiter gentilis, Goshawk, Hønsehauk. 56cm. An uncommon, shy and seldom seen resident which is found in mature forests in the valleys surrounding the mountains. The large nest of twigs is built in the fork of a tree in a secluded place. They hunt by chasing larger songbirds, willow grouse and small mammals. The female is bigger than the male but the plumage is similar. The male hunts for the family during the breeding time.

Pandion haliaetus, Osprey, Fiskeørn. 60cm. A rare visitor now no longer breeding in these mountains but sometimes migrating through. They nest in treetops near lakes from where they hunt fish and, rarely, small mammals. They hunt by plunging feet first into the water to grab a fish. Their breeding areas are towards the extensive forests on the east of the watershed in Norway. During the winter they return mainly to Africa.

Buteo Lagapus, Rough Legged Buzzard, Fjellvåk. 60cm. An uncommon resident in the moorland zone. They nest on craggy ledges in a structure built of twigs. They survive off lemmings and other small rodents, willow grouse and ptarmigan. During a poor lemming year they will not breed. In winter they retreat down to lower altitudes and coastal areas. The sexes are alike and the male feeds the family during breeding.

Aquila chrysaetos, Golden Eagle, Kongeørn. 80cm. A rare resident found in the mountains. They nest on craggy ledges above the tree line, but sometimes treetops also. The nests are a large mass of twigs and are often occupied permanently. The male brings the food for the female and usually two eaglets. They hunt willow grouse, ptarmigan, hare and lemming, and will also eat carrion of lambs, for which they are wrongly blamed for killing.

Nyctea scandiaca, Snowy Owl, Snøugle. 60cm. A very rare resident of open mountainous moorland above the tree line. Although resident they are are nomadic. They nest on the ground atop a hummock on rocky outcrops. During breeding the female is fed on the nest by the male. They subsist primarily on lemmings and in poor lemming years will not breed. The females are slightly larger and darker than the males, which are white.

Bubo bubo, Eagle Owl, Hubro. 70cm. A very rare resident in the wooded valleys around the mountains. They nest on sheltered ledges, crevices or caves on crags and in hollow trees, preferably in a rocky wooded ravine. They hunt at night in more open areas, with prey being small to medium mammals, sometimes up to the size of foxes and young roe deer, and a wide range of birds, including other birds of prey, up to goshawks. The female is larger.

TREES AND SHRUBS OF HURRUNGANE

The Hurrungane massif is partially surrounded by three deep valleys: Bergdalen-Helgedalen, Utladalen and Fardalen. It is only in these valleys that any trees are found. From these three main valley systems there are numerous side valleys. These side valleys are virtually devoid of trees but have a rich covering of scrub.

The three valleys start at the fjords and are initially agricultural. As these deep chasms slice into the mountainous massif the permanent agriculture gives way to pastures used for summer grazing only. Eventually these pastures peter out. Surrounding the agricultural fields and summer pastures are locally managed forests with some naturalized tree speices like Norway spruce. These forests have provided building materials and fuel for centuries.

Above these summer pastures and on the steep and unsuitable slopes around them, like the valley sides, the original woodlands persist. These woodlands are dominated by Scots pine and downy birch with other speices mixed in, especially along stream sides.

Around 600m altitude these forests give way to the mountain birch woods which grow up to 800m. These limits are largely theoretical as the south facing tree lines can be 300m higher than the north facing ones. Above the mountain birch woods are the scrub areas.

The scrub looks the same and is tedious to walk through if there is no path. However, the scrub contains numerous varieties of willow, and also dwarf birch and juniper. In the summer, once the melting snows have exposed these scrub areas, it bursts into life and the young leaves and catkins support a huge quantity and variety of insects. They feed off the plants for nearly 24 hours of productive sunlight and in turn sustain the large numbers of migratory *Passerines* who come to feed off them.

The identification of the willows is a difficult task at any time of year and it is only slightly easier when the catkins are present. If this was not difficult enough, willows are very promiscuous and regularly cross with each other to produce hybrids.

Pinus sylvestris, Scots Pine, Furu. 30m. Pines are common in the surrounding valleys. They grow up to about 750m altitude. They may be many hundreds of years old. Male and the crimson female flowers are borne on same tree in May. The female then develops cones over two years and releases wind borne seeds. Many of the pine trees near Øvre Årdal and Vetti were killed by flouride pollution, but the rest are recovering well.

Populus tremula, Aspen, Osp. 20m. A widespread tree in the valleys around Hurrungane found up to 850m, where it may be just a shrub. They are not shade tolerant. Male and female trees are separate and both bear catkins in May. The fertilized female catkins mature in early summer and the seeds are wind dispersed. They sucker readily from roots, making copses of the same sex. The fluttering leaves turn a warm red in the autumn.

Alnus incana, Grey Alder, Gråor. 10m. Common in the valleys around the massif by water and damp places. They tolerate poor soil but not shade. They grow up to 600m and reproduce by suckers or seeds. The long male and small female catkins appear on the same tree in late summer. They pollinate in March and the female catkins ripen to a small green cone. These become woody and after seed dispersal remain on the tree.

Betula pubescens, Downy Birch, Bjørk. 10m. A pioneer tree, the downy birch is found up to 750m, maybe higher. It prefers damp locations, but will grow anywhere not too arid. It does not tolerate shade so may be crowded out by other speices. The hanging male and erect female catkins appear on the same tree in April. After wind fertilization the female catkins grow, ripen and droop. They release their tiny seeds in late summer.

Picea abies, Norway Spruce, Gran. 35m. Not nearly as widespread as the pine in the surrounding valleys and nearly always introduced or feral. They are found up to 500m and can live for 200 years. The male yellow/purple flowers and female upright purple cones appear in May. These purple cones are fertilized and by October are mature, brown, 12cm cones. The seeds in the cones are shed the following year and wind dispersed.

Sorbus aucuparia, Rowan, Rogn. 10m. A widespread tree which can be found in a variety of habitats up to 850m, sometimes higher. They can tolerate shade. Clusters of white flowers appear in May. The fertilized ones ripen to red berries in August. These berries are attractive to many passerine (song) birds who eat them and disperse the seeds in their droppings. The pinnate leaves turn a rich red in the autumn before falling.

Prunus padus, Bird Cherry, Hegg. 10m. This small tree or bush is found throughout the forested valleys up to 750m. They prefer damp or riparian locations. They often grow in the same locations as grey alder. They are covered in spikes of white flowers in mid May which fertilize themselves and produce small black fruit in August. The fruits, and the stone-like seed, are eaten by birds and dispersed. They do not propagate by suckers.

Betula pubescens ssp. czerepanovii, Mountain Birch, Fjellbjørk. 4m. A hardy tree whose limit is the tree line at about 900m. They grow above the limit of the downy birch, of which they are a sub speices, so share in the reproductive characteristics. They grow very slowly producing a hard but contorted wood. The trees are often infested by insects in the early summer. In the autumn their leaves turn very rich colours before falling.

Betula nana, Dwarf Birch, Dvergbjørk. 0·5m. A small bush which largely occurs above the tree line on moorland up to 1200m, sometimes higher. It is also found by marshes lower down. Reproduction similar to other birches with male and female catkins and then wind dispersal, but also some shoots from root sections. Hosts many insects, and therefore birds, in the summer. The leaves turn rich colours in the autumn.

Myrica gale, Bog Myrtle. Pors. 0·5m. Quite rare in wet and boggy areas in the wooded valleys and rarely growing above 500m. It is an aromatic plant. The 5cm leaves are serrated at the top and narrow to the base. They are dioecious with male and female catkins on different bushes. They appear in May on the previous years shoots with no leaves. The bushes may change sex from year to year. Pollinated by insects, the resulting seeds are wind dispersed.

Salix phylicifolia, Tea-leaved Willow, Grønnvier. 1·5m. Not common but grows in damp stony areas to 1200m. The pointed thick leaves are shiny above and a waxy blue/green under, and are serrated except for the base. Shoots and buds are brown. Leaves and catkins appear at the same time. The bushes are dioecious and catkins are 2-4cm long and erect. Pollination is mainly by insects. The photo is of a female bush.

Salix glauca, Glaucous Willow, Sølvvier. 1m. Very common in damp locations up to 1300m, often higher. These plants are similar to the downy willow but the catkins have small stalks and appear with the leaves, not before. The leaves are 5cm, untoothed and are grey green, but blueish on the underside. They have silky hairs on both sides. The seeds are wind dispersed in autumn, but overwinter under the snow before germinating.

Salix hastata, Halberd-leaved Willow, Bleikvier. 1m. A small bush with thin serrated leaves, which are paler on the underside. Leaves have a hint of red. It is found in wet locations with aluvian soils, such as beside gravelly mountain streams up to 1250m. They are dioecious and the catkins appear in June after the leaves emerge. The catkins are 3-5cm and erect. They are pollinated by insects, and the downy seeds are wind dispersed in August.

Salix reticulata, Net-leaved Willow, Rukkevier. 0·1m. A common shrub found throughout the mountains to 1600m, often higher. It is a creeping plant and roots from the stem as well as producing seeds. The 3cm catkins are borne with the leaves on long stalks once snow has melted in June or as late as July. They are insect pollinated. The 3cm broad leaves are rounded and have a prominent network of veins above and below.

Juniperus communis alpina, Dwarf Juniper, Fjelleiner. 0·5m. A small creeping bush found in rocky, dry places up to 1200m. These very hardy plants grow very slowly and the stems are very strong. The tiny yellow male and female flowers are on separate plants. After fertilization the females flowers take two to three years to ripen into small purple berries. Each berry contains 3-6 seed which get eaten by birds who then disperse them.

Salix caprea, Goat Willow, Selje. 3m. Common in riparian locations in the forested valleys around Hurrungane. They do not grow above the tree line and seldom above 500m. The erect catkins appear before the leaves in April. The larger female catkins may be 7cm, ripen in June and are wind dispersed. The oval leaves have a pointed tip, a dark green upper and a grey downy lower side. The trees play host to many insects in summer.

Salix lapponum, Downy Willow, Lappvier. 1m. Quite common, especially on wet rocky slopes, up to 1300m. These dense bushes bear sessile (without stalks) catkins in late May just before the leaves appear, each sex on its own bush. They are pollinated by insects. The seeds are wind dispersed in late August. The 5cm leaves are oblong and are both dull green-grey and downy on both sides. They are hosts to various insects.

Salix lanata, Woolly Willow, Ullvier. 1m. Unsual in damp locations, up to 1200m. The buds, shoots and oval 5cm leaves are covered in yellowish, silky hairs, but the upper side of the leaf loses these in the summer. The catkins appear before the leaves and are yellow and thick. The bushes are dioecious, the flowers insect pollinated and the seeds wind dispersed. The bushes are similar to and confused with downy and glaucous willows.

Salix myrsinites, Whortle-leaved Willow, Myrtevier. 0·5m. A quite common stiff, knotty bush with small leaves which are shiny on both sides. The leaves are about twice as long as broad and pointed. The previous year's withered leaves are frequently present. The shoots are initially downy. They like wet rocky habitats and grow up to 1300m. They are dioecious and the catkins are 3-5cm long and purplish. The catkins appear with the leaves.

Salix herbacea, Dwarf Willow, Musøyre. 0·02m. A very common mat forming shrub. It is the world's smallest tree at only 2cm! It grows throughout the mountains up to 1800m. They are found in carpets appearing once the snow has melted. Propagates either by a creeping rhizome root sending up aerial shoots or by seeds from ripened 1cm catkins. The leaves are kidney shaped, toothed and a shiny green both sides.

ALGAE, LICHEN & MOSS OF HURRUNGANE

There are too many of these organisms to discuss properly here, so have selected some which are notable. Many of these are lichens.

Lichens are a remarkable relationship between microscopic algal cells and fungal filaments. The lichen body (thallus) is composed of algal cells living inside a compact mass of fungal tissue. The algae provide the fungi with nutrients and the fungi provide the algae with shelter. There are three types of lichens: crustose (crusty), foliose (leafy) and fruticose (shrubby). They are thought to be nutritious for humans but our digestion cannot break them down.

Mosses are found throughout Hurrungane. Most notable are the moss colonies beside rocky tumbling brooks and below large melting snowfields. They are an extreme pioneer spieces.

Chlamydomonas nivalis, Red Snow Algae, Rødsnø algae. This common summer occurence is caused by a blooming algae. The unicellular organism contains chlorophyll to manufacture fuel, but also contains a red pigment which colours them and the snow. In the winter these single celled algae sleep under the snow. In spring they swim up towards the suface in the melting drips to reproduce and synthesize fuel again.

Gallionella ferruginea, Iron Bacterium, Jernbakterier. Where there is some iron dissolved in water (and also some oxygen, carbon and a few other elements present) this bacteria might be found. It lives in the water and oxidizes the iron present to produce fuel for itself. The by-product of this process is ferric hydroxide, an insoluble precipitate which forms the familiar oily coating on the surface of the water.

Rhizocarpon (Various speices), Map Lichen, Kartlav. Very common yellow/green lichen found everywhere in the mountains. It is normally in colonies which often merge, separated by a black band. Once rock has been exposed by a glacier it takes about 20 years to become established and then grows at a rate of 1mm each year. Scientists can therefore use it to measure glacial changes since the mini-ice age 250 years ago. A crustose lichen.

Xanthoria (Various speices), Sunburst Lichen, Raudberglav. This quite comon lichen grows very slowly and requires nitrogen to survive. It therefore thrives on rocks under birds' perches or where animals may defecate. It forms rosettes which are firmly attached to rocks. These lichens grow throughout the mountains on rocks and some varieties may be found on trees also. A crustose lichen.

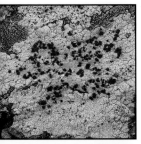

Haematomma ventosum, Wind Lichen, Fokklav. This lichen grows in places which are exposed to the wind and weather. It is a yellow/grey slow growing lichen with blood red specks dotted about it. The red specks protect the lichen from the strong UV radiation, so the higher the lichen, the more red specks. These lichens are strongly attached to the rock and even penetrate into it to get minerals. A crustose lichen.

Umbilicaria (Various speices), Rock Tripe, Navlelav. These lichen are very common on boulders and rock faces throughout the mountains. When the weather is dry they are crispy and increase friction. When wet however they become very slippery and can make the rocks as lethal as verglass. They grow in very exposed environments and are attached to the rock in the centre of their 3-5cm structure. A foliose lichen.

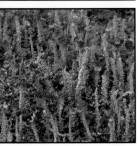

Cladonia bellidiflora, Red Soldier Lichen, Blomsterlav. This fruticose lichen is well known and found in forests, especially coniferous, and moorland areas. The lichen feeds off fallen logs and stumps, breaking them down and putting the nutrients back into the soil. This lichen, like most, also fixes nitrogen from the air and puts it into the soil. The bright red cap is the fruiting body (apothecia) and is formed by the fungal component only.

Cladonia rangiferina, Reindeer Moss, Grå Reinlav. Very common all over the mountains and often found in large colonies in the coniferous, especially pine, forests and drier, stony moorlands. They are greyish 5-10cm high bushes or fruticose lichens. The lichen is slow growing like all lichens. They are a major component of the reindeer diet in the winter months. These lichens were used by humans in dire times, but provide no nutrition.

Cladonia stellaris, Reindeer Moss, Kvitkrull. A very common branched fruticose lichen found throughout the mountains in the same environs as *Cladonia rangiferina*. This lichen has an important economic value as the main winter fodder for reindeer. This lichen was collected in the mountains as a supplementary fodder for cattle also. It is still commercially collected today and exported for decorative uses.

Bryophyta (Various speices), Moss, Mose. There are numerous types of mosses found in the mountains, moorlands and forests of Hurrungane. Most belong to the Musci class and have no roots or vascular tissues, and therefore can only grow in wet conditions where the vegetative parts can absorb water directly. Mosses are usually found in large colonies of plants forming mats beside streams or below large snowfields.

FLOWERS & PLANTS OF HURRUNGANE

There is a wide range of flowers and plants in Hurrungane. Most are perennial. The 138 plants described here are not an exhaustive list. Below is a glossary of terms used in the plant descriptions:

Annual: a plant which completes its life cycle from germination to fruiting, and then death, in a single season. **Biennial:** a plant which complete its life cycle in 2 years, germinating in the first and fruiting and dying in the second. **Perennial:** a plant which survives many years, generally fruiting every year. **Monoecious:** having separate male and female flowers, but on the same plant. **Dioecious:** having seperate male and female plants but borne on different plants. **Rhizome:** a persistant underground creeping stem. **Stolon:** a creeping stem often on the surface growing from the base of erect stems. **Sepal:** often green leaflike scale covering the flower bud and remaing outside the petals. **Calyx:** the collective name for all the sepals. **Alternate:** refers to leaves arising from opposite sides of the stem at regular staggered intervals.

Axil: the angle between the upper side of the leaf and the stem. **Bulbis:** a small bulb-like organ found in the leaf axils on the aerial stems of some plants. **Rosette:** a circular fan of leaves arising from a level, often the base. **Umbel:** an inflorescence in which all the stalks radiate from the same point. **Lanceolate:** lance shaped and widest below middle, usually referring to leaf shape. **Palmate:** leaf with lobes radiating from a common point like a hand. **Lobe:** referring to leaves that are divided but not completely separated by shallow or deep protrusions. **Pinnate:** a leaf with leaflets arranged either side of a common stalk. **Pinnae:** the leaflets of a pinnate leaf. **Pinnule:** a leaflet or a pinnae which is pinnately divided, as on many ferns. **Petiole:** the leaf stalk. **Blade:** the collective leafy components on a fern frond. **Spore:** microscopic body which becomes detached from the parent plant and from which a new plant can develop. Produced in the sporangium on the parent plant.

When referring to the height of a plant the following guide applies;
Low: 1-10cm.   Short: 5-20cm.   Medium: 15-75cm.   Tall: 60-250cm

Polygonum viviparum, **Alpine Bistort, Harerug.** Short. Usual in meadows and screes. Leaves long and thin. White or pink flowers on single stem. Lower flowers replaced by bulbis which falls to form a new plant. This bulbis is rich in starch and edible.

Oxyria digyna, **Mountain Sorrel, Fjellsyre.** Short. Kidney shaped basal leaves, untoothed on long stalks. Flowers are tiny, 4 petalled on branched spikes. Produces winged nut as seed. Common in damp rocky places, below snowfields and beside streams.

Lychnis alpina, **Alpine Catchfly, Fjelltjæreblom.** Short. Leaves linear to spoon shaped, mostly basal. Flowers, usually purple, maybe white, clustered in a small dense head atop a stem. Petals are deeply notched. Common on dry mountain meadows.

Silene wahlbergella, **Northern Catchfly, Blindurt.** Short. Flowers are single on stalk, intially nodding then erect. Leaves narrow and oval. Slightly hairy perennial. The large calyx nearly entirely encloses the flower. Bee pollinated. Rare on moist meadows.

Siliene vulgaris, **Bladder Campion, Engsmelle.** Medium. Greyish hairless perennial with erect stems and all shoots flowering. Flowers white with deeply notched petals. Calyx inflated but not all encompassing. Leaves elliptical. Dry, grassy and rocky areas.

Silene acaulis, **Moss Campion, Fjellesmelle.** Low. A mosslike cushion of up to 25cm. The small 5 petal flowers cover this cushion in the summer. The flowers on short stalks are pink, maybe white. Common on damp gravel, moraine, and turf.

Silene dioica, **Red Campion, Jonsokblom.** Medium. A hairy plant with erect stems. The leaves are oblong. These plants are dioecious with the pink 5 petalled male and female flowers each found on their own plant. Found in birch woods, meadows and moorland.

Stellaria borealis, **Northern Starwort, Fjellstjerneblom.** Short. Creeping plant with smooth square stems. Leaves linear to oval. Flowers solitary and few, often with white petals missing. Found in rocky birch woods and willow scrub where they are rare.

Stellaria nemorum, **Wood Stitchwort, Skogstjerneblom.** Medium. Leaves oval with tip pointed. Lower leaves long-stalked. Stem hairy. White flowers with 5 petals deeply clefted, almost to base. Common in moist birch woodlands and beside streams.

Sagina saginoides, **Alpine Pearlwort, Seterarve.** Low. Hairless perennial with rosettes of linear leaves up stem and at base. Flowers solitary or 2 on stem, with white petals the same length as green sepals. Common in damp rocky, and gravelly places.

Cerastium cerastoides, **Starwort Mouse-ear, Brearve.** Low. A loosly matted creeping plant with flowering stems. The leaves are small and linear, curving to one side. White flowers with 5 deeply notched petals on sticky stalks. Common on damp moorlands.

Cerastium alpinum, **Alpine Mouse-ear, Fjellarve.** Low. A mat forming perennial with oval leaves and erect stems with flowers. Stem and leaves hairy. White flowers with 5 clefted petals. Petals twice the length of sepals. Found on rocky moorland and ledges.

Minuartia biflora, **Two-flowered Sandwort, Tuearve.** Low. A slender, tufted, slightly hairy perennial with narrow linear leaves. The white flowers are usually single but may be up to 3 on a stem. Found on damp moorland meadows and often by large melting snowfields.

Trollius europaeus, **Globe Flower, Ballblom.** Medium. Tufted hairless perennial with deep cut leaves with 3-5 serrated lobes. Flowers with at least 10 incurved petals. Flower often single, sometimes 2-3 on stem. Rare on damp meadows and mountain pastures.

Aconitum septentrionale, **Wolf's bane, Tyrihjelm.** Tall. Found in colonies growing from tuberous stock. The hollow hairy stems bear multiple purple flowers at top. Leaves with 7-8 lobes, clefted to midrib. Common in birch woods. The plants are poisonous.

Pulsatilla vernalis, **Spring Pasque Flower, Mogop.** Short. A hairy perennial with white purple tinged flowers on a single stem. After flowering stem lengthens. The leaves are lobed. Common on mountain meadows near snow in late May/June. Poisonous.

Ranunculus acris, **Meadow Buttercup, Engsoleie.** Medium. A variable, hairy perennial with leaves deeply divided into 3-7 wedge shaped lobed segments. Flowers golden yellow with 5 petals. Common on grassy areas and birch woods. Poisonous.

Ranunculus pygmaeus, **Dwarf Buttercup, Dvergsoleie.** Low. Small hairless perennial with unbranched stems. Kidney shaped leaves with 3-5 lobes. Yellow flowers with 5 petals and hairy sepals. Common by melting snowfields on mountain moorlands.

Ranunculus hyperboreus, Arctic Buttercup, Setersoleie. Low. Creeping or floating perennial, almost hairless. Leaves are oval and 5 lobed. The yellow flowers have 3, rarely 4, flowers and sepals. Common in wet places on rocky moorlands. Poisonous.

Thalictrum alpinum, Alpine Meadow-rue, Blåsprett. Short. Delicate perennial with slender stem. Small rounded leaflets on low wispy branches. Flowers violet with brown pendant anthers. Unusual on damp turf in rocky areas and ledges. Inconspicious.

Arabis alpina, Alpine Rockcress, Fjellskrinneblom. Low. A hairy creeping perennial with flowering stems. Leaves are oval and toothed, mostly basal. The flowers are white and clustered atop stem. Fruit in 25mm pods. Common in high, damp, rocky areas.

Rhodiola rosea, Roseroot, Rosenrot. Short. Hairless tufted perennial with alternate fleshy leaves on erect stems. The flowers are yellow. Flower sexes on different plants (dioecious). Plant becoming red in autumn. Common in wet, rocky mountain areas.

Saxifraga nivalis, Alpine Saxifrage, Snøsildre. Short. Sticky hairy perennial with thick oblong toothed leaves in a basal rosette. Leaves underside reddish. White or pink flowers on top of crowded stem. Common on shaded rock ledges, moraines and screes.

Saxifraga cespitosa, Tufted Saxifrage, Tuesildre. Low. Cushion forming, hairy perennial with mostly 3 lobed leaves in a basal rosette. Clusters of 1-3 flowers on a slightly leafy stem. 5 petalled flowers are white to cream. Unusual on drier ridges and screes.

Saxifraga oppositifolia, Purple Saxifrage, Rødsildre. Low. A mat forming perennial with trailing stems covered in small oval opposite leaves. Solitary stalkless purple flowers appearing early summer. Common on wet, rocky mountain slopes and screes.

Dryas octopetala, Mountain Avens, Reinrose. Low. Downy evergreen undershrub. Sometimes old. Leaves oblong toothed; green above, white and felt-like below. White, 8 petalled flowers on long stalks. Found on dry, rocky moorland, where it may be common.

Ranunculus platanifolius, Large White Buttercup, Kvitsoleie. Tall. A slightly hairy tufted perennial with tall erect stems. Leaves palmate with 5-7 lobes and long-stalked. Flowers white with petals falling easily. Damp woodlands.

Cardamine bellidifolia, Alpine Bittercress, Høyfjellskarse. Low. A hairless perennial with thick spoon shaped leaves mostly in a basal rosette. White flowers in clusters of 2-5 atop stem. Fruit is a browning 25mm pod. Common on wet gravel and by late snowfields.

Sedum annum, Annual Stonecrop, Småbergknapp. Low. Hairless annual or biennial plant with stems from base. Leaves alternate, oblong and fleshy, often reddish. Yellow short-stalked flowers. Unusual in mountains in rocky areas.

Parnassia palustris, Grass-of-Parnassus, Jåblom. Short. Hairless tufted perennial with heart shaped leaves, mostly long-stalked basal, but some on stems. White 5 petal flowers solitary on long stems. Common on moist moorlands and mountain riparian areas.

Saxifraga adscendens, Ascending Saxifrage, Skåresildre. Short. Hairy robust biennial. Most leaves on basal rosette where they are unstalked and wedge shaped. White flowers on branched stem in small clusters. Unusual on dry mountain pastures and screes.

Saxifraga cernua, Drooping Saxifrage, Knoppsildre. Short. Erect perennial with single stem. Basal leaves kidney shaped with 5-7 lobes. Stem leaves unlobed and unstalked, with red bulbis in axils. White flower atop stem. Common on moist, shady rocky slopes.

Saxifraga cotyledon, Mountain Queen. Bergfrue. Medium. A perennial with large basal rosette of oval, succulent, blunt (but pointed tip) leaves. Many small white flowers on a 40cm branched stem. Unusual on rocky ledges, crevices and stable moraines.

Geum rivale, Water Avens, Enghumleblom. Short. Tufted hairy perennial with 3-6 pairs of rounded deep lobed leaflets. Cream to dull pink nodding flowers with puple calyx. Flowers born on lax stems. Rare in moist birch woodlands and beside shady streams.

Ranunculus glacialis, Glacier Buttercup, Isoleie. Low. Hairless perennial with deeply lobed fleshy basal leaves. The 5-8 petalled flowers are white initially then tinted with purple, usually single on stalks. Very common in rocky/gravel areas by late snowfields.

Arabis hirsuta, Hairy Rock Cress, Bergskrinneblom. Short. A variable hairy biennial with lanceolate leaves mostly in a basel rosette. Clusters of white flowers usually atop stem. Fruit is 25mm pod wth seeds inside. Rare on wet rocks, but usual in dry habitats.

Sedum villosum, Hairy Stonecrop, Lodnebergknapp. Low. Reddish, hairy perennial with erect flowering stems and small fleshy leaves. Flowers lilac and long-stalked. Reproduces with a bulbis on stem by leaf stalk. Unusual on wet rocky mountain terrain.

Saxifraga stellaris, Starry Saxifrage, Sternesildre. Short. Hairy tufted perennial with oval toothed leaves in basal rosette. Stout branched stem with small clusters of white flowers atop. Petals have 2 yellow spots near base. Very common in damp mountain areas.

Saxifraga aizoides, Yellow Mountain Saxifrage, Gulsildre. Short. Slightly hairy perennial with small fleshy oblong leaves. Flowers are 5 petalled, yellow/orange, maybe with red spots. Sepals bit shorter than petals. Rocky wet moorland and scrub.

Saxifraga rivularis, Brook Saxifrage, Bekkesildre. Low. Tufted perennial with creeping stolons. Leaves kidney shaped with 3-5 lobes on long stalks. A bulbis at base of these stalks. White flowers in clusters of 1-3. Common by water and melting snowfields.

Rubus chamaemorus, Cloudberry, Molte. Short. A creeping hairy perennial with annual stems from rhizome body. Leaves kidney shaped, rough and lobed. Flowers white and monoecious. Some years female rests. Fruit is prized berry. Common on upland bog.

Potentilla nivea, Snow Cinquefoil, Snømure. Medium. Tufted hairy perennial with trifoliate leaves with oval toothed leaflets. Yellow flowers on lax branched clusters. The 5 petals slightly longer than the sepal. Rare on dry rocky slopes, screes and morraines.

***Potentilla erecta*,
Tormentil, Tepperot.**
Low. Creeping downy
perennial. Leaves with
3-5 leaflets, silvery below.
Stem leaves unstalked
and basal withering
soon. Yellow flowers
in lax clusters, mostly
4 petalled. Unusual in
meadows and grassy
moorland.

***Fragaria vesca*,
Wild Strawberry,
Markjordbær.** Low.
A perennial with long
rooting runners and
trifoliate toothed leaves.
White flowers in lax
clusters bear small edible
red berry. Unusual on
drier grassy slopes, and
by disturbed areas.

***Anthyllis vulneraria
ssp.lapponica*, Kidney
Vetch, Fjellrundbelg.**
Short. A variable silky
haired perennial with
pinnate leaves with 5-15
leaflets. Yellow or orange
flowers in dense clusters.
Fruit is a wind dispersed
pod. Common on drier
stony mountain areas.

***Geranium sylvaticum*,
Wood Cranesbill,
Skogstorkenebb.**
Medium. Tufted perennial
with toothed 5-7 lobed
leaves divided to near
base. Pairs of purplish
flowers with whiter
centre and darker veins.
Common in birch woods
and willow scrub.

***Epilobium
anagallidifolium*,
Alpine Willowherb,
Dvergmjølke.** Low. A
creeping perennial with
leafy stolons and small
opposite oval leaves.
Pale purple flowers
on lax stem. Common
throughout mountains in
wet habitats like
snowfields.

***Cornus suecica*, Dwarf
Cornel, Skrubbær.**
Short. A rhizomous
perennial with erect
unbranched stems. The
leaves are opposite and
oval. The flower, atop
the stem, is a cluster of
purple heads surrounded
by 4 white bracts. Fruit is
red berry. Woodland and
moorland.

***Urtica dioica*,
Common Nettle,
Storenesle.** Tall. A
perennial with stolons
and square stems. Leaves
heart shaped, toothed
and armed with stinging
hairs. Plants are dioecious
with catkin males and
clustered female flowers.
Unusual on disturbed or
near cultivated ground.

***Empetrum
hermaphroditum*,
Crowberry,
Fjellkrekling.** Short.
Mat forming subshrub
with evergreen linear
leaves. Tiny flowers in
leaf axils ripen into an
edible black berry. Very
common on exposed
high moorland up to
1700m.

***Potentilla crantzii*,
Alpine Cinquefoil,
Flekkmure.** Short.
Hairy perennial with
woody stock. Leaves
palmate with 5 oblong
toothed leaflets. The 2cm
yellow 5 petal flowers
borne in lax clusters,
often have an orange
spot near base. Common
in rocky areas.

***Alchemilla vulgaris*,
Lady's Mantle,
Marikåpe.** Medium. An
aggregate of a few similar
species of perennials
with kidney shaped
leaves, with 5-11 lobes.
Small yellow flowers in
dense clusters. Common
on wet moorland,
snowfields and mountain
streams.

***Astragalus alpinus*,
Alpine Milk-vetch,
Setermjelt.** Short.
Hairy perennial with
slender stems on which
are pinnate leaves with
7-12 pairs of elliptical
leaflets. Flowers white
with blue purple tint.
Fruit is an oblong pod.
Common on drier
mountain meadows.

***Viola biflora*, Yellow
Wood Violet, Fjellfiol.**
Low. Fragile, slightly hairy
perennial with kidney
shaped leaves, most in
basal tuft. Yellow flowers
with brown veins, usually
in pairs on stem with
smaller leaves. Common
in damp wooded and
scrub areas.

***Epilobium alsinifolium*,
Chickweed
Willowherb,
Kjeldemjølke.** Short.
A slightly hairy perennial
with long spreading
stolons. Leaves mostly
opposite, toothed and
oval. Purple flowers atop
stem with some leaves.
Common in mountains
by wet areas and brooks.

***Angelica sylvestris*,
Wild Angelica, Sløke.**
Tall. A robust hairless
perennial with hollow
stems. Lower leaves 2-3
pinnate, oblong toothed
segments. Small white
or pink flowers in 20cm
umbels, soon falling.
Fruit tiny nut with wings.
Common in damp woods
and meadows.

***Pyrola minor*,
Common
Wintergreen,
Perlevintergrøn.** Short.
A perennial with toothed,
tough oval leaves and
stalk. Round white to pink
flowers on erect stem.
Common in mountains
on damp moorland, birch
woods and willow scrub
habitats.

***Cassiope hypnoides*,
Matted Cassiope,
Moselyng.** Low.
Subshrub with slender
moss-like stem. White,
often with a pink tint,
nodding flowers borne
on slender stems. Very
common throughout
the mountains in damp
locations, like snowfields.

***Sibbaldia procumbens*,
Creeping Sibbaldia,
Trefingerurt.** Low.
Hairy perennial with
woody stock. Leaves
trifoliate and basal
and dead leaves often
attached. Small clusters
of yellow/green flowers,
needing a few years to
develop. By snowfields
and wet moorland.

***Alchemilla alpina*,
Alpine Lady's Mantle,
Fjellmarikåpa.** Short.
A woody stock perennial
with leaf stems ending
in leaf rosette with
5-7 deep lobes. Small
yellowish petalless
flowers clustered on
stem. Common on wet
mountain areas and by
melting snowfields.

***Lotus corniculatus*,
Birdsfoot Trefoil,
Tiriltunge.** Short.
Sprawling woody based
perennial with pinnate
leaves with 3-5 rounded
leaflets. Yellow to orange
flowers in clusters. Fruit
a 25mm straight pod.
Common in meadows
and drier moorland
areas.

***Epilobium
angustifolium*,
Rosebay Willowherb,
Geitrams.** Tall. Robust,
hairless, patch forming
perennial with alternate
lanceolate leaves. A
spiked cluster of purple
flowers. Wind dispersed
seeds in a pod. Common
on rocky areas, especially
if disturbed.

***Epilobium hornemannii*
Hornemann's
Willowherb,
Setermjølke.** Short.
A creeping perennial
with short underground
stolons in rosette. Leaves
thin, green, with trace
of red. Flowers are a
pale violet. Common in
mountains by wet areas.

***Angelica archangelica*,
Angelica, Fjellkvann.**
Tall. A stout hollow stem
perennial with toothed
diamond shaped leaves.
Small cream or green
flowers in 25cm umbels.
Fruit small and oblong
with wings. Fragrant.
Common in birch woods
and wet moorland.

***Diapensia lapponica*,
Lapland Diapensia,
Fjellpryd.** Low.
A cushion forming
evergreen perennial
subshrub. Small, tough,
spoon shaped leaves.
White 5 petal, 15mm
flowers. Fruit a dry
capsule with many seeds.
Likes drier exposed
mountain ridges.

***Rhododendron
lapponicum*, Lapland
Rosebay, Lapprose.**
Medium. Spreading
evergreen undershrub.
Leaves oblong and green
with rusty underside.
Purple flowers develop
early in clusters. Rare on
exposed dry moorland
in north east of
Hurrungane.

Vaccinium oxycoccos, Cranberry, Stortranebær. Low. A small creeping evergreen subshrub with oval untoothed leaves, green above, whiteish below, 3-6mm wide. Flowers pink to red. Red 8-10mm berry. Common in wet mossy woods and heaths.

Vaccinium uliginosum, Bog Bilberry, Blokkebær. Tall. An erect deciduous shrub with oval untoothed green/blue leaves. Flowers white with pink tint and bell shaped. Berry is blue/black, 7-10mm and edible. Common in coniferous woods and damp moorland areas.

Arctostaphylos uva-ursi, Bearberry, Mjølbær. Short. An evergreen shrub with long rooting branches. Leaves alternate, green, oval and leathery. Flowers are white to pink in terminal clusters. Red 6-8mm edible berries, but tasteless. Drier rocky moors and open woods.

Phyllodoce caerulea, Blue Mountain Heath, Blålyng. Short. Heather-like evergreen shrub with stems rooting at base. The tiny leaves are oblong and alternate. Pink nodding bell shaped flowers. Fruit a dry capsule. Common on rocky moorlands, avoiding exposed sites.

Polemonium caeruleum, Jacob's Ladder, Fjellflokk. Medium. A tuft forming perennial with erect stems covered in 8-12 pairs of alternate lanceolate leaves. Blue 20-30mm flowers in dense terminal clusters. Unusual on damp, rocky meadows.

Gentianella campestris, Field Gentian, Bakkesøte. Short. Erect biennial with a branched stem and oval leaves. Purple flowers sometimes pale, have 25mm long tubes, 4 lobed openings and are clustered atop stem. Common on drier heaths and moorland areas.

Veronica fruticans, Rock Speedwell, Bergveronika. Medium. A tufted perennial with branched stems and a woody stock. Leaves oval, but narrow, untoothed and scarcely stalked. Blue flowers in terminal clusters. Common on rocky mountain slopes.

Pedicularis oederi, Oeder's Lousewort, Gullmyrklegg. Short. An erect, hairless, semi-parasitic perennial. Pinnately lobed leaves. Yellow flowers (upper lip has crimson tip) clustered in dense spike atop stem. Common on mountain heaths and grasslands.

Vaccinium microcarpum, Small Cranberry, Småtranebær. Low. A subshrub similar to *Vaccinium oxycoccos* but the leaves only 2.5mm wide and the red berry 5-8mm wide. Also edible. Common in the drier regions of wet mossy woods and boglands.

Vaccinium myrtillus, Bilberry, Blåbær. Medium. A creeping deciduous shrub with oval green, toothed leaves. The solitary reddish flowers are lantern shaped. Berry is blue/black when ripe and edible. Common in coniferous woods, dry birch woods and heaths.

Arctostaphylos alpinus, Mountain Bearberry, Rypebær. Low. Creeping shrub with toothed leaves which turn rich crimson in autumn. White flowers appear early and produce a red then black 6-10mm edible but tasteless berry. Common overall above tree line on heathland.

Primula scandinavia, Scandinavian Primrose, Fjellnøkleblom. Short. A perennial with hairy oblong leaves in a basal rosette. Slightly hairy erect stem bears a cluster of 2 to 10 purple flowers with yellow centre. Quite rare on drier rocky heath and high meadow slopes.

Gentiana purpurea, Purple Gentian, Søterot. Medium. Perennial with unbranched erect stems bearing oval lanceolate leaves. Purple flowers mostly in clusters atop stem but also in leaf axil on stem. Unusual in rocky birch woods, willow scrub and meadows.

Myosotis decumbens, Mountain Forget-me-not, Fjellminneblom. Short. A hairy branched perennial with creeping stolons and oval basal leaves and some lanceolate stem leaves. Blue flowers in clusters. Common in mountain grasslands and birch woods.

Euphrasia frigida, Cold Eyebright, Fjellaugnetrøst. Low. A semiparasitic annual. Feeds off roots of other plants. Toothed, hairy, oval, short stalked leaves. The white flowers have a lilac tint and yellow centre. Common overall on damp mountain heaths.

Pedicularis lapponica, Lapland Lousewort, Bleikmyrklegg. Short. A largely hairless, semi parasitic perennial with straight stems and pinnately lobed leaves. Cream yellow flowers horizontally spread atop stem. Usual in dry and damp mountain heaths.

Vaccinium vitis-idaea, Cowberry, Tytebær. Low. Prostrate creeping subshrub with oblong untoothed leaves with margins rolled under. Flowers are pink and bell shaped. The red berry is 5-10mm and is edible but bitter. Common in woods, scrub and moors.

Andromeda polifolia, Bog Rosemary, Hvitlyng. Medium. An evergreen shrub with alternate long leaves with margins rolled under. Pink bell shaped nodding flower in terminal clusters. Fruit is a erect capsule. Unusual in boggy areas and acid soil, not above treeline.

Loiseleuria procumbens, Trailing Azalea, Greplyng. Low. A mat forming subshrub with small evergreen oblong leaves. Pink flowers, nodding as buds, in small terminal clusters or solitary. Common on exposed moorland ridges with little snow cover.

Trientalis europaea, Chickweed Wintergreen, Skogstjerne. Short. A hairless perennial with a creeping rootstock. Leaves often in a single whorl near stem top. The white flowers with 5-9 petals are starry and sometimes pink tinged. Usual in damp woods.

Gentiana nivalis, Snow Gentian, Snøsøte. Low. A slender annual herb with erect stems and unstalked oval leaves. Intense blue flowers have a narrow tube and open lobes which close when temperature dips below +10 celcius. Common in birch woods and moorland.

Veronica alpina, Alpine Speedwell, Fjellveronika. Short. A slightly hairy perennial with oval unstalked leaves and erect stems. Small blue flowers in terminal clusters, closing in wet weather. Common on moist rocky mountain meadows and by brooks.

Bartsia alpina, Alpine Bartsia, Svarttopp. Short. A hairy perennial with erect stems which is semiparasitic on grasses. Leaves oval, toothed and unstalked and are purple towards top. Flowers are dark purple atop stem. Very common on damp mountain meadows.

Pinguicula vulgaris, Common Butterwort, Tettegras. Low. A perennial overwintering as a bud at ground level. Fleshy oblong leaves are sticky and trap insects which are then digested. Solitary blue flower atop short stem. Very usual on wet heaths and moorland.

HURRUNGANE: FLOWERS & PLANTS

***Campanula rotundifolia*, Harebell, Blåklokke.** Short. A stoloniferous, hairless perennial with erect stems. Leave are linear and few. The 3cm, blue, bell shaped flowers are nodding and solitary atop stem. Common in mountains on dry grassy habitats.

***Erigeron borealis*, Alpine Fleabane, Fjellbakkestjerne.** Short. A hairy perennial with basal oval stalked leaves and lanceolate unstalked stem leaf. Often solitary flowers with yellow disc with white to purple rays. Common in mountains on rocky, grassy habitats.

***Antennaria alpina*, Alpine catsfoot, Fjellkattefot.** Short. Similar to *Antennaria dioica*, but the bracts of both male and female flowers are grey brown, and the flower heads smaller. Male plants are very rare. Common on drier heaths.

***Petasites frigidus*, Lapland Butterbur, Fjellpestrot.** Medium. A rhizomous perennial with stems bearing heart shaped leaves and flowering leafless stems. The dioecious plants have 5-15 pink (male) or cream (female) clustered flowers. Wet boggy areas.

***Cicerbita alpina*, Alpine Sow-thistle, Turt.** Tall. A creeping perennial with a stout hollow stem. The large leaves are pinnately lobed with triangular ends. Flowers are 20mm with blue disc and ray, and are clustered atop stem. Common in damp birch wood and grassy scrub.

***Tofieldia pusilla*, Scottish Asphodel, Bjønnbrodd.** Short. A hairless perennial with tufts of swordlike basal leaves. The white/green flowers are borne atop stem in spiked cluster of 5-10. Common through out in damp mountain and heath habitats.

***Coeloglossum viride*, Frog Orchid, Grønnkurle.** Short. A tuberous rooted perennial with 2-5 oval leaves decreasing in size up stem. Flowers on lax spike green/yellow tinged with purple. Usual in moist grassy heathland and birch wood habitats.

***Dryopteris expansa*, Northern Buckler Fern, Sauetelg.** Medium. A perennial with 100cm frond. Petiole third leaf length. Blade 3 cut and lacy. Pinnae oblong with basal small. Pinnules toothed. Spores 1mm in 2 rows under pinnule. In moist woodland.

***Solidago virgaurea*, Goldenrod, Gullris.** Medium. A variable perennial with oblong stalked basal leaves and linear unstalked stem leaves. The flowers have a yellow disc (centre) and yellow rays (outer) in clusters atop stem. Very common throughout the mountains.

***Erigeron uniflorus*, Dwarf fleabane, Snøbakkesterne.** Low. Hairy perennial with stalked spoon shaped basal leaves and few stem leaves. Solitary flower with yellow disc and white to pale lilac ray. Common by snowbeds and on mountain pasture.

***Omalotheca supina*, Dwarf Cudweed, Dverggråurt.** Low. A hairy creeping perennial with lanceolate leaves and stems with rayless brown flowerheads. These may be in clusters of 2-7. Common in snowbeds and damp rocky mountain meadows.

***Saussurea alpina*, Alpine sawort, Fjelltistel.** Short. A stoloniferous perennial with alternate lanceolot leaves. Purple flowerheads in a cluster of 3-15 atop stem. Vanilla scented flowers. Common on wet, rocky, grassy moorland, birch woods and willow scrub.

***Leontodon autumnalis*, Autumn Hawkbit, Følblom.** Short. A slightly hairy perennial with a basal rosette of linear, deeply toothed leaves. A solitary 25mm yellow flower atop stem which contains milk. Common on grassy snowbeds and birch woods and willow scrub.

***Convallaria majalis*, Lily-of-the-valley, Liljekonvall.** Medium. A patch forming poisonous perennial with 2-3 large green oval leaves. White, fragrant, bell shaped flowers on a stem which ripen into red berries. Unusual in the wooded valleys and meadows.

***Gymnadenia albida*, Small-white Orchid, Kvitkurle.** Short. Hairless tuber-rooted perennial with a stem 2-3 basal sheaths and narrow leaves. Pale cream fragrant flowers in dense spike. Usual on grassy habitats in mountain heaths and birch woods.

***Erigeron acer*, Blue Fleabane, Bakkestjerne.** Medium. A variable, hairy annual or biennial with erect branched stems. Leaves are oval to lanceolate, basal stalked and stem unstalked. Flowers with yellow disc and lilac/white ray. Usual by birch woods and scrub.

***Antennaria dioica*, Catsfoot, Kattefot.** Short. A creeping perennial with a basal rosette of spoon shaped and downy undersided leaves. Dioecious plants with terminal clusters of 3-8 flowers with white (male) or pink (female) bracts. Common on drier heaths.

***Omalotheca norvegicum*, Highland Cudweed, Setergråurt.** Short. A downy perennial with lanceolate leaves. Dark flowerheads found clustered on the stem by leaf axils and atop stem. Common in birch forests, scrub, heath and melting snowbeds.

***Cirsium helenioides*, Melancholy Thistle, Kvitbladtistel.** Medium. A perennial with stout, often unbranched stems which are leafless at the top. Purple, or rarely white, usually solitary flowerheads atop stem. Damp meadows, birch woods and scrub.

***Heiracium alpinum*, Alpine Hawkweed, Fjellsveve.** Short. Hairy perennial with spoon shaped leaves in a basel rosette. A 25mm solitary yellow flower atop stem usually with small single leaf on stem. Common in mountains on rocky ridges and heaths.

***Chamorchis alpina*, False Orchid, Fjellkurle.** Low. A tuberous rooted perennial with 4-8 linear erect basal leaves. Flowers in a short spike and green/yellow tinged with purple/brown. Petals and sepals closed to form a hood. Unusual on damp grassy mountain heaths.

***Gymnadenia conopsea*, Fragrant Orchid, Brudespore.** Short. A tuberous perennial with 2-3 basal sheaths and 4-8 linear leaves on stems, the uppermost smallest. Pink, purple or rarely white fragrant flowers in dense spikes. Common in grassy woods in heaths.

***Polystichum lonchitis*, Holly-fern, Taggbregne.** Medium. An evergreen perennial with stiff 50cm fronds. Petiole an eighth of leaf length. Blade 1 cut and narrow. Pinnae triangular, toothed and spiny. No pinnules. Spores in 2 rows under pinnae. In rocky woodlands.

***Cystopteris fragilis*, Brittle Bladder Fern, Skjørlok.** Short. Delicate perennial with 30cm fronds. Petiole black at base. Blade 3 cut, narrow and lacy. All but upper pinnae equal length. Pinnules with round lobes. Spores under these lobes. Damp rocky places.

Athyrium filix-femina, Lady Fern, Skogsburkne. Medium. A perennial with a 100cm lacy frond. Petiole tan with dark scales. Blade elliptic, 2 cut and wide at middle. Pinnae short stalked and lanceolate. Pinnule deeply cut. Spore under pinnule. Damp woods and rocks.

Athyrium distentifolium, Alpine Lady Fern, Fjellburkne. Medium. A perennial with 70cm frond. Petiole ¼ blade length with basal scales. Blade outline lanceolate and 3 cut. Pinnae sessile. Pinnule deeply cut. Spore under pinnule. Damp rocky heath, above trees.

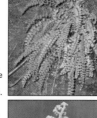

Asplenium viride, Green Spleenwort, Grønburke. Short. A tufted perennial with 15cm fronds. Blade linear and 1 cut. Pinnae round, toothed with short stalks. Pinnules none. Spores under pinnae near midrib. Common overall on rocky habitats.

Cryptogramma crispa, Parsley Fern, Hestespreng. Short. A perennial with lacy 20cm, 3 cut fronds. The plants have infertile fronds with flat pinnules as in photo and fertile fronds with incurved pinnule margins covering the spores. Screes and heath.

Pteridium aquilinum, Braken, Einstape. Tall. A rhizomous perennial with 100cm+ lacy, 3 cut fronds. Pinnae triangular. Pinnule linnear with deeply toothe lobes. Spores under inrolled pinnule margins. Common in all woodland and drier rocky slopes.

Botrychium lunaria, Moonwort, Marinøkkel. Short. A rhizomous perennial with a single stem. Stem divided into a fertile branched spike with pendant clusters of spores and infertile leaf with fan shaped pinnae. Usual, but overlooked, on drier mountain meadows.

Huperzia selago, Fir Clubmoss, Lusegras. Low. An evergreen rooted perennial with a tuft of vertical stems. Sharp leaves cover stem in 8 rows. Spores in the axils of the upper leaves. Some bulbis on stems also. Poisonous. Common from forest to tundra.

Selaginella selaginoides, Lesser Clubmoss, Dvergjamne. Low. An evergreen creeping perennial with upright cone bearing soft leaves. Spores sit in the axil of the leaves. Leaves have tiny hairs on margin. Common in wet grassy habitats and moorland.

Lycopodium alpinum, Alpine Clubmoss, Fjelljamne. Low. Creeping perennial with upright stems covered in 4 ranks of leaves. In fertile stems spores in leaf axil at top. In sterile stem leaf pressed to stem. Very common in mountains and down to upper forest.

Equisetum sylvaticum, Wood Horsetail, Skogsnelle. Medium. A rhizomous perennial with 2 stems; fertile with cone atop which matures, droops and falls before stem becomes sterile with 10-25 whorled levels of drooping branches. Usual in woods.

Luzula spicata, Spiked Wood-rush, Aksfrytle. Short. A tufted perennial with mostly basal, grooved, 1-2mm wide, slightly hairy leaves. Flowers/fruit in dense drooping cluster atop stems, with horizontal spike above cluster. Usual in drier mountain areas.

Juncus triglumis, Three-flowered Rush, Trillingsev. Short. A tufted perennial with stiff stems and narrow leaves mostly basal, but 1 on low stem sometimes. Mostly 3, but maybe 2-5, brown to yellow flowers with all 3 at same level atop stem. Unusual on wet gravels.

Juncus trifidus, Three-leaved Rush, Rabbesev. Short. A tufted perennial with short thin basel sheath-like leaves. Stem is leafless until flower when 2-3 long leaf-like bracts extend up past the dark flowers, which are in clusters of 1-3. Usual by stony areas in mountains.

Carex bigelowii, Stiff Sedge, Stivstorr. Short. A rhizomous perennial with stiff sharp angled stems. Dark male spike, usually single atop stem, with 2-3 dark unstalked 5-15mm female spikes below. Similar to Common Sedge. Very usual throughout mountains.

Carex norvegica, Alpine Sedge, Fjellstorr. Short. A tufted perennial with sharply 3 sided stems and leaves 3-5mm wide. The dark flowers are atop the stem in 2-4 unstalked egg shaped spikes. The lower spike is the male. Quite usual in moist, grassy, stony mountain habitats.

Carex atrata, Black Sedge, Svartstorr. Medium. A perennial with tufts, solitary sharp 3 sided stem and 4-10mm wide leaves. Flowers atop stem in nodding spikes, male below and 2-4 females above. A leaf-like bract grows past spikes. Usual in high meadows.

Carex flava, Yellow Sedge, Gulstorr. Medium. A tufted perennial with 4-7 mm wide leaves often longer than stem. Flowers are single narrow male spike above 2-4 unstalked wider female spikes. Usual in damp hillside and forest habitats.

Carex lachenalii, Hare's-foot Sedge, Rypestorr. Short. Loosely tufted perennial with bluntly 3 sided, stiff stem. Narrow leaves. Flowers in 3-4 spikes atop stem with the females above the male spike at base of cluster. Common in damp heaths and wet mountain areas.

Eriophorum scheuchzeri, Arctic Cotton-grass, Snøull. Medium. Rhizomous perennial with rounded solitary stems and narrow leaves. Solitary spike on stem emerges from an inflated sheath and ripens to fruit with woolly bristles. Common in wet areas.

Phleum alpinum, Alpine Cat's-tail, Fjelltimotei. Short. Tufted perennial with flat leaves and inflated sheaths. Stem often with 2 leaves. The 4cm long panicle (spike-like flower cluster) atop stem is oval and purplish. Usual in mountains, liking damp areas.

Anthoxanthum odoratum, Sweet Vernal Grass, Gulaks. Short. A tufted perennial with smooth flat leaves and stems topped by a dense brown spike of flowers, which appear in the early summer. The grass is aromatic when dried. Very common.

Deschampsia alpina, Alpine Hair-grass, Fjellbunke. Medium. A tufted perennial with a spreading flower cluster and narrow, sometimes inrolled leaves. The flowers do not produce seeds but a bulbis which falls and roots. Common in damp gravel habitats.

Trisetum spicatum, Northern Oat-grass, Svartaks. Medium. A tufted perennial with hairy leaves and erect downy stems topped with a dark spike-like flowerhead, sometimes not continuous. Fairly common in rocky and gravel mountain habitats.

Poa alpina, Alpine Meadow Grass, Fjellrapp. Medium. A tufted perennial with 4mm wide leaves and a loose pyramidal flowerhead with purple tinted spikelets. In the mountains more likely to produce bulbis than flowers. Very common.

APPENDIX: SCANDINAVIAN MOUNTAINS AND PEAKS OVER 2000M

There are 137 mountains, and 102 secondary peaks, over 2000m in Scandinavia. These are found in 20 different regions. The regions are Hurrungane, Jotunheimen, Breheimen, Reinheimen, Rondane, Dovre, Sarek and Kebnekaise. Jotunheimen, however, is subdivided into another 13 massifs. There follows a list of all these regions, their mountains and the secondary peaks on them.

For this book I have taken the definition of a mountain to be that where there must be at least 100m of vertical ascent from the highest saddle. Anything lower than this is a secondary top. Secondary tops with 30m or more of vertical ascent from the highest saddle are classed as peaks, while those with less than 30m are unclassified. Please refer to page 9 for a more detailed explanation. The diagram to the right might help to clarify this also.

HURRUNGANE (JOTUNHEIMEN)		
1.1	**Store Skagastølstind**	**2405m**
1.15	Vetle Skagastølstind	2340m
1.16	Midtre Skagastølstind	2284m
1.17	Skagastølsnebbet	2222m
1.18	Nordre Skagastølstind	2167m
1.2	**Styggedalstind**	**2387m**
1.3	**Gjertvasstind**	**2351m**
1.4	**Sentraltind**	**2348m**
1.19	Maradalstind	2160m
1.5	**Austanbotntind**	**2204m**
1.20	Søre Austanbotntind	2103m
1.21	Vestre Austanbotntind	2100m
1.6	**Dyrhaugstind**	**2147m**
1.22	Søre Dyrhaugstind	2072m
1.23	Nordre Midtmaradalstind	2062m
1.7	**Store Ringstind**	**2124m**
1.8	**Soleibotntind**	**2083m**
1.24	Søre Soleibotntind	2049m
1.25	Nordre Soleibotntind	2030m
1.9	**Fannaråken**	**2068m**
1.10	**Midtmaradalstind**	**2056m**
1.11	**Stølsmaradalstind**	**2026m**
1.12	**Steindalsnosi**	**2025m**
1.13	**Midtre Ringstind**	**2025m**
1.14	**Østre Ringstind**	**2002m**

STØLSNOS MASSIF (JOTUNHEIMEN)		
2.1	**Stølsnostind**	**2074m**
2.2	**Falketind**	**2067m**
2.3	**Østre Stølsnostind**	**2001m**

URANOS MASSIF (JOTUNHEIMEN)		
3.1	**Uranostind**	**2157m**
3.5	Søre Uranostind	2048m
3.6	Slingsbytind	2026m
3.2	**Mjølkedalspiggen**	**2040m**
3.3	**Sagi**	**2040m**
3.4	**Langeskavlstind**	**2014m**

RAUDDALEN AREA (JOTUNHEIMEN)		
4.1	**Store Rauddalseggi**	**2168m**
4.2	**Skarddalseggi**	**2159m**
4.3	**Store Rauddalstind**	**2157m**
4.4	**Snøholstind**	**2141m**
4.5	**Mjølkedalstind**	**2138m**
4.6	**Skarddalstind**	**2110m**
4.7	**Austre Rauddalstind**	**2068m**
4.8	**Midtre Høgvalgtind**	**2066m**
4.9	**Vestre Rauddalstind**	**2059m**
4.10	**Midtre Rauddalseggi**	**2016m**

VISBRETIND (JOTUNHEIMEN)		
5.1	**Visbretind**	**2234m**
5.7	Langvasshøi	2030m
5.2	**Semelholstind**	**2147m**
5.6	Sørvestre Urdadalstind	2080m
5.8	Nordre Semelholstind	2004m
5.3	**Store Urdadalstind**	**2116m**
5.4	**Midtre Urdadalstind**	**2060m**
5.5	**Kyrkja**	**2032m**

SLETTMARK-MESMOG MASSIF (JOTUNHEIMEN)		
6.1	**Mesmogtind**	**2264m**
6.2	**Langedalstind**	**2206m**
6.3	**Kvitskardstind**	**2193m**
6.4	**Slettmarkshø**	**2190m**
6.5	**Svartdalspiggen**	**2165m**
6.10	Nordre Svartdalspiggen	2137m
6.12	Midtre Svartdalspiggen	2065m
6.13	Søre Svartdalspiggen	2065m
6.6	**Slettmarkspiggen**	**2163m**
6.14	Slettmarkskampen	2032m
6.7	**Østre Torfinnstind**	**2119m**
6.8	**Midtre Torfinnstind**	**2110m**
6.11	Vestre Torfinnstind	2085m
6.9	**Galdeberget**	**2075m**

APPENDIX: SCANDINAVIAN MOUNTAINS AND PEAKS OVER 2000M

KALVEHØGDI MASSIF (JOTUNHEIMEN)

7.1	**Kalvehøgdi**	**2208m**
7.4	Østre Kalvehøgdi	2178m
7.5	Leirungskampen	2079m
7.2	**Rasletind**	**2105m**
7.6	Østre Rasletind	2010m
7.3	**Nordre Kalveholotind**	**2019m**

KNUTSHOLS-TJØNNHOLS MASSIF (JOTUNHEIMEN)

8.1	**Knutsholstind**	**2341m**
8.10	Nordre Knutsholstind	2185m
8.11	Midtre Knutsholstoind	2170m
8.2	**Tjønnsholstind**	**2331m**
8.7	Høgdebrotet	2226m
8.13	Eggi	2041m
8.3	**Austre Leirungstind**	**2288m**
8.6	Skarvflyløyfttind	2250m
8.8	Søre Skarvflytind	2210m
8.12	Midtre Skarvflytind	2154m
8.4	**Vestre Leirungstind**	**2250m**
8.9	Vesle Knutsholstind	2205m
8.5	**Tjønnholsoksle**	**2145m**

SMØRSTABB MASSIF (JOTUNHEIMEN)

9.1	**Storebjørn**	**2222m**
9.2	**Smørstabbtind**	**2208m**
9.3	**Saksi**	**2189m**
9.13	Peak north of Saksi	2077m
9.21	Geite	2002m
9.4	**Loftet**	**2170m**
9.5	**Veslfjelltind**	**2157m**
9.6	**Veslebjørn**	**2150m**
9.12	Skeii	2118m
9.16	Kalven	2034m
9.7	**Kniven**	**2133m**
9.8	**Gravdalstind**	**2113m**
9.15	South west Smørstabbtind	2045m
9.17	South Smørstabbtind	2033m
9.18	South east Smørstabbtind	2030m
9.9	**Bakarste Skagsnebb**	**2093m**
9.20	Skagsnebb	2003m
9.10	**Veslbretind**	**2092m**
9.14	Hurrbretind	2060m
9.19	Storbretind	2018m
9.22	Jervefonni	2001m
9.11	**Stetind**	**2020m**

Visbretind rises up from a crevassed glacier. The north ridge (right) is a classic scramble.

GALDHØPIGGEN MASSIF (JOTUNHEIMEN)

10.1	**Galdhøpiggen**	**2469m**
10.2	**Skardstind**	**2373m**
10.20	North east of Skardstind	2175m
10.3	**Vesle Galdhøpiggen**	**2369m**
10.16	Galdhøi	2283m
10.18	Kjelhøi	2223m
10.4	**Storgjuvtind**	**2344m**
10.14	Ymelstind	2304m
10.5	**Bukkehøi**	**2314m**
10.21	Vestre Bukkeholstind V1	2166m
10.22	Vestre Bukkeholstind V2	2166m
10.23	Vestre Bukkeholstind V4	2166m
10.24	Vestre Bukkeholstind V3	2161m
10.28	Lindbergtind	2120m
10.6	**Store Tverråtind**	**2309m**
10.15	Midtre Tverråtind	2302m
10.19	Svellnosbrehesten	2181m
10.7	**Storgrovhøi**	**2259m**
10.17	Nordre Storegrovhøi	2253m
10.8	**Store Bukkeholstind**	**2213m**
10.25	Østre Midtre Bukkeholstind	2154m
10.27	Vestre Midtre Bukkeholstind	2135m
10.30	Søre Bukkeholstind	2058m
10.9	**Styggehøi**	**2213m**
10.10	**Store Tverrbotntind**	**2161m**
10.26	Nordre Midtre Tverråtind	2151m
10.29	Søre Midtre Tverråtind	2106m
10.11	**Nordre Bukkeholstind**	**2149m**
10.12	**Vestre Tverrbotntind**	**2113m**
10.13	**Tverrbytthornet**	**2102m**

Store Bukkeholstind has a fine north west ridge.

APPENDIX: SCANDINAVIAN MOUNTAINS AND PEAKS OVER 2000M

The jagged ridge of Store Memurutind. The east top (left) is 2m higher than the west.

MEMURU-VEO MASSIF AREA (JOTUNHEIMEN)

11.1	**Surtningssui**	**2368m**
11.14	Sortopp Surtningssui	2302m
11.22	Søre Blåbrehøi	2196m
11.2	**Store Memurutind**	**2366m**
11.15	Vestre Memurutind V1	2280m
11.16	Vestre Memurutind V3	2243m
11.19	Vestre Memurutind V4	2230m
11.26	Vestre Memurutind V6	2140m
11.3	**Store Heillstugutind**	**2345m**
11.4	**Midtre Heillstugutind**	**2339m**
11.21	Nordre Heillstugutind	2218m
11.27	Nordre Heillstugubrehesten	2136m
11.28	Søre Heillstugubrehesten	2120m
11.30	Heillstuguhøi	2072m
11.5	**Leirhøi**	**2330m**
11.23	Veobrehesten	2185m
11.6	**Austre Memurutind**	**2301m**
11.7	**Søre Veotind**	**2267m**
11.17	Store Veotind	2240m
11.18	Sørøstre Styggehøbretind	2232m
11.20	Sørvestre Styggehøbretind	2220m
11.24	Nordre Styggehøbretind	2167m
11.25	Nordre Blåbrehøi	2165m
11.29	Nordre Veotind	2120m
11.8	**Nestsøre Heillstugutind**	**2255m**
11.9	**Semeltind**	**2236m**
11.10	**Søre Heillstugutind**	**2189m**
11.11	**Veobretind**	**2189m**
11.12	**Hinnotefjell**	**2114m**
11.13	**Spiterhøi**	**2033m**

The Heillstugu ridge lies in the heart of Jotunheimen.

SJØDALEN (JOTUNHEIMEN)

12.1	**Nautgardstind**	**2258m**
12.4	Østre Nautgardstind	2194m
12.5	Nautgardsoksli	2089m
12.2	**Besshøi**	**2258m**
12.3	**Stornubben**	**2174m**
12.6	Nordøstre Stornubben	2049m

Store Urdadalstind rises above the invigorating river in Visdalen.

GLITTERTIND MASSIF (JOTUNHEIMEN)

13.1	**Glittertind**	**2452m**
13.7	Østre Glittertindoksli	2260m
13.11	Glitter-Rundhøi	2089m
13.2	**Trollsteinseggi**	**2300m**
13.3	**Trollhøi**	**2201m**
13.8	Steinhøi	2161m
13.9	Gråhøi	2154m
13.10	Østre Trollhøi	2090m
13.4	**Trollstein-Rundhøi**	**2170m**
13.12	Svartholshøi	2067m
13.5	**Ryggehøi**	**2142m**
13.6	**Grotbrehesten**	**2018m**

Storebjørn is one of the most characteristic mountains in the alpine Smørstabb massif.

KVITINGSKJØLEN (JOTUNHEIMEN)

14.1	**Østre Kvitingskjølen**	**2064m**
14.2	**Vestre Kvitingskjølen**	**2060m**

APPENDIX: SCANDINAVIAN MOUNTAINS AND PEAKS OVER 2000M

BREHEIMEN		
15.1	**Store Hestbrepigg**	**2172m**
15.2	**Midtre Hestbrepigg**	**2160m**
15.15	Vest Midtre Hestbrepigg	21-3m
15.16	Østre Hestbrepigg	2132m
15.19	Låven	2012m
15.3	**Vestre Hestbrepigg**	**2139m**
15.4	**Hestedalshøgdi**	**2091m**
15.5	**Tverrådalskyrkja**	**2088m**
15.17	Søre Tverrådalskyrkja	2034m
15.18	Sorvest for Fortunsdalsbreen	2018m
15.6	**Lodalskapå**	**2083m**
15.7	**Vestraste Hestbrepigg**	**2078m**
15.8	**Lomseggi**	**2068m**
15.9	**Midtre Holåtind**	**2047m**
15.10	**Moldurhøi**	**2044m**
15.11	**Austre Holåtind**	**2043m**
15.12	**Vestre Holåtind**	**2039m**
15.13	**Hesthøi**	**2021m**
15.14	**Brenibba**	**2018m**

Lodalskåpa is a steep nunatak on the edge of the huge Josterdalsbreen icesheet.

REINHEIMEN		
16.1	**Gråhø**	**2014m**

RONDANE		
17.1	**Rondslottet**	**2178m**
17.2	**Storronden**	**2138m**
17.9	Vinjeronden	2044m
17.3	**Høgronden**	**2114m**
17.4	**Midtronden**	**2060m**
17.10	Østre Midtronden	2042m
17.5	**Sagtind**	**2018m**
17.6	**Storsmeden**	**2016m**
17.7	**Veslesmeden**	**2015m**
17.8	**Digerronden**	**2015m**

DOVRE		
18.1	**Snøhetta**	**2286m**
18.7	Midttoppen	2278m
18.8	Hettpiggen	2261m
18.9	Vesttoppen	2253m
18.2	**Svånåtind**	**2209m**
18.11	Nordre Svånåtind	2004m
18.3	**Larstind**	**2106m**
18.4	**Østre Langvasstind**	**2085m**
18.10	Vestre Langvasstind	2046m
18.5	**Skredahøin**	**2004m**
18.6	**Bruri**	**2001m**

Sarektjåhkkå with the south ridge on the left and the difficult north east ridge on the right.

SAREK		
19.1	**Sarektjåhkkå**	**2089m**
19.5	Nordtoppen	2056m
19.6	Sydtoppen	2023m
19.7	Bucht-toppen	2010m
19.2	**Áhkká**	**2015m**
19.3	**Bårddetjåhkkå**	**2005m**
19.4	**Balgatttjåhkkå**	**2002m**

KEBNEKAISE		
20.1	**Giebmegáisi ***	**2104m**
20.4	Nordtoppen	2097m
20.2	**Gaskkascohkka**	**2076m**
20.3	**Gaskkasbákti**	**2043m**

* At the moment the south top is higher but the north top will be soon.

Gaskkasbákti has no easy route. The east ridge (hidden from view) is grade III and the classic south west ridge (on the left) is grade IV.

Idyllic vistas are around every corner in the foothills of Hurrungane.

Smørstabbtind, 2208m, rises steeply out of the glacier in the massif to the east of Hurrungane.

HURRUNGANE (JOTUNHEIMEN)

1.1	**Store Skagastølstind** (Storen)	**2405m**	
	1.15	Vetle Skagastølstind	2340m
	1.16	Midtre Skagastølstind	2284m
	1.17	Skagastølsnebbet	2222m
	1.18	Nordre Skagastølstind	2167m
1.2	**Styggedalstind**	**2387m**	
1.3	**Gjertvasstind**	**2351m**	
1.4	**Sentraltind**	**2348m**	
	1.19	Nordre Maradalstind	2160m
1.5	**Austanbotntind**	**2204m**	
	1.20	Søre Austanbotntind	2103m
	1.21	Vestre Austanbotntind	2100m
1.6	**Dyrhaugstind**	**2147m**	
	1.22	Søre Dyrhaugstind	2072m
	1.23	Nordre Midtmaradalstind	2062m
1.7	**Store Ringstind**	**2124m**	
1.8	**Soleibotntind**	**2083m**	
	1.24	Søre Soleibotntind	2049m
	1.25	Nordre Soleibotntind	2030m
1.9	**Fannaråken**	**2068m**	
1.10	**Midtmaradalstind**	**2056m**	
1.11	**Stølsmaradalstind**	**2026m**	
1.12	**Steindalsnosi**	**2025m**	
1.13	**Midtre Ringstind**	**2025m**	
1.14	**Østre Ringstind**	**2002m**	

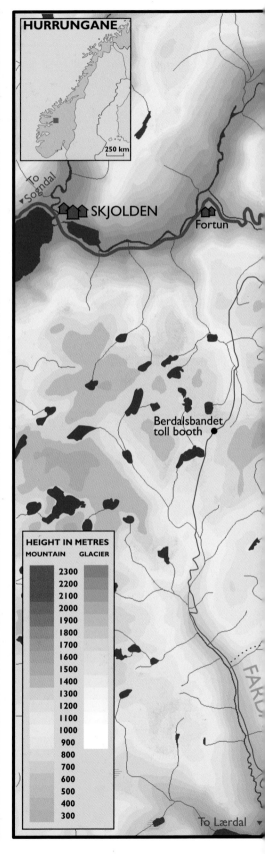

HURRUNGANE

250 km

To Sogndal

SKJOLDEN

Fortun

Berdalsbandet toll booth

HEIGHT IN METRES

MOUNTAIN   GLACIER

2300
2200
2100
2000
1900
1800
1700
1600
1500
1400
1300
1200
1100
1000
900
800
700
600
500
400
300

FARD

To Lærdal